PLAYING TENNIS AFTER 50

Kathy and Ron Woods

HUMAN KINETICS

Library of Congress Cataloging-in-Publication Data

Woods, Kathy.
 Playing tennis after 50 / Kathy and Ron Woods.
  p. cm.
 Includes bibliographical references and index.
 ISBN-13: 978-0-7360-7244-1 (soft cover)
 ISBN-10: 0-7360-7244-6 (soft cover)
 1. Tennis for older people. I. Woods, Ron, 1943 Nov. 6- II. Title.
 GV1001.4.A35W66 2008
 796.342--dc22

                            2008017283

 ISBN-10: 0-7360-7244-6
 ISBN-13: 978-0-7360-7244-1

The Web addresses cited in this text were current as of July 2008, unless otherwise noted.

Acquisitions Editor: Laurel Plotzke; **Developmental Editor:** Cynthia McEntire; **Assistant Editor:** Scott Hawkins; **Copyeditor:** Annette Pierce; **Proofreader:** Jim Burns; **Indexer:** Dan Connolly; **Graphic Designer:** Robert Reuther; **Graphic Artist:** Tara Welsch; **Cover Designer:** Keith Blomberg; **Photographer (cover):** Jupiter Images/Creatas/Alamy; **Photographer (interior):** Neil Bernstein, unless otherwise noted; **Photo Asset Manager:** Laura Fitch; **Photo Office Assistant:** Jason Allen; **Art Manager:** Kelly Hendren; **Associate Art Manager:** Alan L. Wilborn; **Court Diagrams:** Tammy Page; **Cartoons:** Ben Boyd; **Printer:** United Graphics

We thank the Racquet Club of St. Petersburg in St. Petersburg, Florida, for assistance in providing the location for the photo shoot for this book.

Human Kinetics books are available at special discounts for bulk purchase. Special editions or book excerpts can also be created to specification. For details, contact the Special Sales Manager at Human Kinetics.

Printed in the United States of America   10 9 8 7 6 5 4 3 2 1

Human Kinetics
Web site: www.HumanKinetics.com

United States: Human Kinetics
P.O. Box 5076
Champaign, IL 61825-5076
800-747-4457
e-mail: humank@hkusa.com

Canada: Human Kinetics
475 Devonshire Road Unit 100
Windsor, ON N8Y 2L5
800-465-7301 (in Canada only)
e-mail: info@hkcanada.com

Europe: Human Kinetics
107 Bradford Road
Stanningley
Leeds LS28 6AT, United Kingdom
+44 (0) 113 255 5665
e-mail: hk@hkeurope.com

Australia: Human Kinetics
57A Price Avenue
Lower Mitcham, South Australia 5062
08 8372 0999
e-mail: info@hkaustralia.com

New Zealand: Human Kinetics
Division of Sports Distributors NZ Ltd.
P.O. Box 300 226 Albany
North Shore City
Auckland
0064 9 448 1207
e-mail: info@humankinetics.co.nz

PLAYING TENNIS AFTER 50

CONTENTS

ACKNOWLEDGMENTS

Playing Tennis After 50 would not have become a reality without the initial support and backing of Rainer Martens, whose friendship and support for years has allowed us to work with the Human Kinetics team on numerous books and videos.

The staff at Human Kinetics is truly professional in their roles. Cynthia McEntire, developmental editor, has been thorough, prompt, and insightful every step of the way. Laurel Plotzke, acquisitions editor, led us expertly through the initial steps of development and continued her support throughout the project. Photographer Neil Bernstein added his genius and personality to the successful photo shoot. Kudos to artists Ben Boyd and Tammy Page for the cartoons and diagrams, respectively, and to Jackie Keller for the team championships photo.

We are indebted to our home club, the Racquet Club of St. Petersburg, a member-owned and family-oriented tennis facility in Florida, for allowing us to use their venue for the photo shoot. The models in the photos graciously volunteered to portray the necessary shots. We are grateful to club president Ben Godwin as well as Shelia and Nick Routh, Diana and Marshall Craig and granddaughter Julia, Earl and Pat Gehant, Marty and Elaine Normile, Dana and Robert Vicander, Don and Maria Drew, and Lisa Grattan. All the senior men and women of the Racquet Club provide daily inspiration through their continuing avid tennis play.

The enthusiastic support of Prince Tennis, led by Doug Fonte, has been terrific. Peg Connor provided tennis rackets, balls, and equipment for the photos. We also appreciate their continuing support through the marketing and sales effort.

Various USTA staff, including Anne Davis, Paul Lubbers, Rick Rennert, Glenn Arrington, Laura Canfield, and consultant Sandy Coffman, have provided materials and encouragement along the way.

Finally, we both salute the thousands of tennis players we have played with, taught, and coached over the years, especially those over age 50. We used to marvel at their love for the game, dedication to fitness, and savvy court strategy. Now we've joined that eminent group and gratefully enjoy playing tennis more than ever.

No project like this could succeed without the understanding and encouragement of family. We are grateful for their love, especially our daughters Nikki and Renee.

INTRODUCTION

Age 60 is the new 40, the age that marks the onset of middle age, according to many pundits. Just think—you are in the prime of your life and you want to enjoy it. If you are a typical person over the age of 50, you are eager to stay healthy and maintain physical strength and vigor, you want to enjoy socializing with people like yourself, and you want to look and feel good. Tennis can help you achieve every one of those goals.

In the United States, nearly 80 million people, out of a population of 300 million, are over 50. That's the largest percentage of older adults in history, thanks to the baby boomers. Medical science has done its part by helping to prolong life so that the average life expectancy is well into the 70s and 80s. Even 100-year birthday celebrations are becoming common. But what do we do for the last 25 years or more of life when working days are over, children move away, and retirement looms?

Surveys that track recreational sports show that many Americans are heading to the gym to use treadmills, elliptical trainers, strength training machines, or stationary bicycles. A significant number, especially women, have opted for yoga or Pilates. But indoor gyms, where the message is "work out," don't appeal to everyone. Over time, many drop out of fitness clubs because people struggle to discipline themselves.

On the other hand, some physical activities are more like play, and tennis is one of them. The sheer pleasure of playing can produce intense feelings of enjoyment, success, fun, and delight. Hitting a solid shot for a winner, ending a point with a well-placed volley, or making an impossible save create feelings of exultation.

Our friends who play golf report some of the same experiences, but it takes them at least four hours to play a round compared to an hour or two for tennis. Time on a tennis court is less expensive than time on a golf course, tennis courts are more accessible, and the equipment is significantly more affordable. And tennis boasts nearly equal participation by both genders. By comparison, golfers are 85 percent male. According to studies on sports participation from the Sporting Goods Manufacturers Association, tennis participation is up 8 percent over the past seven years, while golf has declined 14.2 percent during the same time.

Tennis players do not all have the same reasons for playing the sport. No one over age 50 plays in the hopes of becoming a professional player or a world champion. However, some do like to compete at the highest level they are capable of within their age group. Others prefer friendly social games with people they enjoy spending time with and sharing food or drink after play. Still others use tennis as their primary physical activity to boost their energy, burn calories, increase endurance, and manage their weight. Some families have discovered that tennis can be a dynamic family activity that bridges generations by sharing a common passion for the sport.

Many tennis players embrace the challenge of a skill sport and constantly seek to expand their repertoire of shots and polish the existing ones. Of course there are the brainy players who enjoy the mental challenge of outthinking an opponent tactically and countering his or her every move. We also have legions of tennis friends who simply enjoy hitting the ball repeatedly, whether it is against a rebound wall, a ball-feeding machine, or a hitting partner. Their joy comes from striking the ball and getting physical on the court. Many of these folks claim that tennis is their stress reliever and a powerful physical outlet.

Whatever your motivation to play tennis, we've presented the game in a way that will help you reach your personal goals. There is no one right way to play tennis except (in our view) to enjoy it. It should be fun for you and for your partners and opponents because after all, it really is just a game.

You also might be interested to know that the major reasons people cite for not playing tennis are not having time, having no one to play with, and poor skills. These three barriers far outnumber any others. Keep them in mind as you read through this book. Choosing the right tennis facility and periodically enlisting the expert help of a teaching professional are keys to overcoming these barriers. Likewise, our approach to understanding the strategy and tactics of the game first will speed your learning of the stroke techniques you need because the purpose will be clear and obvious. And last, joining group lessons, socializing after play, and joining tennis groups will smash the perceived barrier of a lack of partners or opponents.

If time has been a barrier for you, reprioritize your time allocation every day. By age 50, many of your former time demands are a memory, and if your health and fitness occupy a more significant role in your values, spending time on the tennis court just makes good sense. It's fun, healthy, and challenging and allows you to be playful. And a tennis court is full of lively, energetic people.

But what about you? What's your story? Is tennis already a major feature of your lifestyle? Maybe you used to play and dropped out at some point. Or perhaps you have never played but have always admired those who did play, and you've decided to give it a try. No matter your story, we want you to love the game like we do and hope our enthusiasm rubs off on you as you read and reread this book.

This book addresses the needs of new tennis players, lapsed tennis players, and continuing players. Whatever your previous participation or skill level, you will find solid advice, suggestions, techniques, and insights into making tennis a part of your life.

If you are thinking about starting to play tennis, you may be unsure how to go about it and perhaps confused about what to expect. We offer you clear, concrete suggestions for choosing the right tennis facility and advice for learning to rally the ball consistently so you can have fun and be physically active. We also present the basic strategic ideas for both doubles and singles play so you will understand how to play the sport. If learning fundamental tennis technique is your aim, we suggest key points for each stroke and recommend that you join an instructional group so you can learn, practice your skills, and make new friends that may become tennis partners or opponents. Don't overlook chapter 10, which contains a wealth of information on tennis equipment. This advice will help you get off to the best start by pointing you toward equipment that is current, affordable, and gives you the best chance of success. Forget that old tennis racket in the closet that has gathered dust. It simply won't work the way you want it to.

This book will also help the lapsed tennis player, one who used to play tennis but stopped as work, family, children, and time took priority. You have been thinking about getting back to the sport but your goals for playing tennis probably have changed from those in your earlier days. You'll be particularly fascinated by the chapters on doubles and singles strategy because you may not have had much experience with those concepts during your former tennis years. The information on stroke technique will help you brush up your strokes so they are more efficient and effective. Be sure to also check out the chapters devoted to keeping your body healthy and in shape so you can avoid setbacks and injury timeouts that can be frustrating just when you are starting to enjoy playing. Like someone new to tennis, you also should invest in up-to-date tennis equipment. Better rackets with larger heads and sweet spots will increase the odds that you'll play better than ever.

If you are a continuing player who has loved tennis and played it all your life, you want to continue to play even as age catches up with you. Creaky joints, sore muscles, and diminishing skills can present a daily challenge. To stay in the game, carefully read chapter 11, Body Talk, so you can stay injury free and fit for tennis. You'll also want to consider our advice in the chapters on doubles and singles strategy for adjusting your tactical play as your mobility decreases. Chapters 6 and 9 on doubles and singles technique will help you polish your on-court skills and perhaps inspire you to add a new shot or two to your repertoire. If your mind and emotions keep getting in the way of your tennis performance, chapter 3 will help you adjust your attitude toward competition and suggest techniques for combating anxiety, nerves, and choking.

To help you interpret the strategic principles, we've divided tennis players into two main groups based on the National Tennis Rating Program (NTRP). (For a more complete description of the NTRP levels, visit www.usta.com/adultseniorleague. Click on "Find your suggested NTRP level.") The first group includes players who are rated at NTRP level 3.0 and lower. This group includes players who are just beginning through those who play a fairly respectable game at the club or recreational level. A player at the NTRP 3.0 level is reasonably consistent during play and usually hits shots at a medium pace (the speed of the ball off the racket). When these players try to change the direction of the shot, add depth, or hit with power, they often experience at least one significant stroke weakness and an overall lack of control on most shots. If you play at level 3.0 or lower, it is key that you carefully read chapter 4 on basic doubles strategy and adopt the fundamental positioning, strategy, and tactics that are recommended.

The second group of players, who are rated at NTRP 3.5 and higher, are classified as intermediate to advanced players. These are savvy tennis players who have been playing for some time and can execute basic strategy during play. A player at the NTRP 3.5 level has dependable stroke execution on most shots hit with moderate pace, but still lacks depth and variety. Typically this player exhibits more aggressive net play, covers the court well, and has a sense of teamwork when playing doubles. If your rating is 3.5 or above, your rating is higher because you've added consistency, depth, placement, and power to most of your strokes. You also have the ability to formulate a game plan and adjust it to your particular opponents. You would benefit from reviewing chapters 6 and 9, which focus on stroke technique, to see if you can fine-tune your game or perhaps add a new shot. A must-read for you is chapter 5, Advanced Doubles Strategy and Tactics, where you'll find nuggets of wisdom to help you raise your level of play.

Let's take a quick look at the overall organization of the four parts of the book and their content. Depending on your tennis experience and skill level, you may want to jump right to chapters that are most relevant for you. Other readers will want to begin with chapter 1 and move methodically through the text. Whatever your preference, we want to emphasize that our approach is for you to understand the basic principles of strategy and tactics before you worry about stroke technique. Once you've absorbed the strategic principles, you'll see why you need to be able to execute certain shots with consistency accuracy, and appropriate placement. We hope to convince you that power is not the key to tennis, although it sure does feel good to hit the ball hard if you choose the right time.

Part I sets the stage for playing better tennis by helping you identify the key reasons you play and providing advice for choosing where to play. We'll also highlight the changes in play most players make after age 50, and we'll carry that concept through the succeeding chapters. This part will also focus on the physical dimension of tennis play, including advice for better rallying skills, trying Cardio tennis, and supplementing tennis with other physical activities to build overall fitness. Finally, in this part, we'll tackle the challenges of tennis competition, put it in a better perspective, and guide you with specific suggestions for controlling your nerves and combating pressure when winning and losing counts.

Part II is all about doubles play because this is the game of choice for the majority of players over age 50. In fact, even among club and recreational players from ages 25 to 50, doubles play is more popular than singles. This book is different from most tennis books because it begins with a presentation or review of the basic strategy and tactics for doubles before discussing stroke technique. Our experience shows that if you understand and learn the strategic concepts first, you'll enjoy learning and readily see the need to improve stroke technique. Chapter 4 lays out the basic strategy for doubles, and chapter 5 takes strategy to the next level as the skill level rises. Even if you're at the 3.0 NTRP level of play, it is worth a peek at chapter 5 just to see what you're aiming for if you want to improve your play. In chapter 6, we'll spend time on the technique for the shots that are especially important in doubles play, how to correct typical technique errors, and advice for practicing doubles play. You'll begin to see that playing tennis doubles clearly presents different challenges than playing singles and requires different stroke technique and the ability to play as part of a team. Chapter 7 is dedicated to those brave souls who dare to play mixed doubles. We say that tongue in cheek because we love playing mixed, but have also seen sad cases of mixed teams who simply misunderstand how to enjoy tennis together. Whether your mixed partner is your significant other or not, understanding the differences between the mixed game and same-gender doubles will save your relationship and open up a new world of tennis fun.

Part III will help you understand the strategy, tactics, and stroke technique for singles play. We'll show you how singles differs from doubles in most respects yet maintains certain principles that transfer from one game to the other. For some players, singles is their fitness workout, and they love the test of individual competition. You'll learn which shots have the best percentage of success in each situation and typical patterns of play for developing a point. Because you're past age 50, adjustments in both strategy and technique may be in order. And we'll also present advice on how to develop your own style of play.

In part IV we address off-court issues such as choosing the best tennis rackets, balls, strings, shoes, and clothing. If you're going to play your best, you need to have the right stuff and a bag to carry it in. Chapter 11 is required reading if you want to properly take care of your body and play tennis for years to come. We've outlined our best advice and included information from experts in sports medicine to help you warm up and cool down properly; prevent injuries through better tennis technique; and improve your overall strength, flexibility, and balance. And in the event that all that advice goes for naught, we've described a team of health care professionals that can help get you back on the court fast. Finally, in chapter 12 we offer suggestions for incorporating regular tennis play into your lifestyle. As people's lives change over the decades, they reinvent themselves and seek new adventures, passions, and entertainment. Tennis can help link your family together or provide the focus for travel or vacation to watch or to play.

Throughout the book are sidebars titled Stroke Doctor. Each of these is based on our experience in helping thousands of players diagnose and cure typical problems in tennis technique. We hope they help, but if you're still not satisfied, we recommend that you schedule time with a certified tennis professional.

In relevant chapters, we also offer practice tips to help you improve your tennis skills with time-tested drills or modified games. If you've fallen into the trap of simply playing tennis without practicing your skills, chances are your play has reached a plateau. If you dedicate just half an hour a week to improving your skills, we're sure you will see returns.

At the end of each chapter is a section called Words to the Wise. These quick chapter summaries will help you check your understanding of the content and remember it. If the concepts are not immediately clear, perhaps rereading that section in the chapter will be helpful.

We've had an exciting and rewarding journey in our tennis lives. Both of us got our start in serious tennis play during college and turned that experience and passion into a lifetime of teaching, coaching, and sharing tennis with others. Our goal is to keep doing that, and we hope you'll join us in playing tennis well beyond the age of 50. We plan to do just that.

KEY TO DIAGRAMS

X	Bounce of ball
A, B, C, D	Players
$\boxed{1}$, $\boxed{T}$	Target
- - - $\langle\!\!-\!\!\rangle$ - - ➤	Path of ball
⟶	Path of player
- - - - - - ➤	Possible angle of return by opponent
⤴	Lob
$\textcircled{A_1}$	Initial position
$\boxed{A_2}$	Second position
$\triangle A_3$	Third position
A_1 , A_2	Possible positions

Take It to the Court

If you're over age 50, you already are aware of some of the effects of aging on life in general and specifically on physical activity and tennis play. The good news is that through proper training and care of the body, you can delay the effects of aging for years. The bad news is that you can't put off aging forever, so you have to adjust your game. The information in this book will help you do just that. We'll share surefire ways to counteract the effects of aging so you can enjoy tennis like never before.

Research studies consistently have shown that people who regularly participate in physical activity maintain relatively higher levels of physical fitness and ability in spite of the passage of time. Playing tennis regularly will help you maintain flexibility, reaction time, strength, balance, coordination, mobility, and overall health. If you add in a few complementary activities, you can enjoy an active lifestyle through the eighth decade of life and perhaps beyond.

According to the World Health Organization, "Research shows that physical activity promotes general well-being, overall physical and psychological health, and independent living. In addition, it ameliorates specific diseases common in later life and reduces the impact of many disabling and painful conditions" (Payne and Isaacs 2005, p. 439).

Some of you are already convinced that tennis is the sport for you, but you wonder how many more years you can play. Others are willing to give it another try after years without playing, and some of you may be thinking about trying something new. Part I will help you think through your personal options, clarify your reasons for playing tennis, and start the process of playing happily for decades to come.

In chapter 1, we tackle the issue of where to play, helping you choose a location that fits your preferences, reasons for playing tennis, and pocketbook. We help you understand the value of support from a tennis teaching professional, finding tennis partners, and building a social network of tennis friends. You'll also confront the reality of playing tennis after age 50 and begin to see the possibilities rather than the barriers.

Chapter 2 focuses on the physical side of tennis. From learning how to rally consistently to using tennis as a primary fitness activity, you'll see the physical side of the game. We believe that tennis is a terrific physical activity, but admit that it is not a perfect prescription for a complete fitness program, and we suggest supplemental activities to keep your body moving smoothly and efficiently.

Chapter 3 switches to the mental and emotional side of tennis. Particularly if you enjoy the challenge of competition, you'll have to handle the thoughts and emotions that often get in the way of playing well. You will learn to deal with the anxiety that comes from playing with pressure during competition by adopting a mature perspective and acquiring the skills to control your mind and emotions.

CHAPTER 1

The Game Past 50

Whatever your previous experience has been with tennis, it's time to take a look at how playing tennis can help shape your life in the future. The good news is it is clear that you can happily play tennis through your early 90s! But you first need to clarify your expectations for playing tennis before you head to the courts. Our goal is to encourage you to figure out a plan to make tennis a key part of your recreational life so it satisfies the expectations you set for yourself.

Research studies by AARP show that turning 50 is one of the most significant triggers for peaking interest in physical activity. When people reach that milestone birthday, they often take stock of their health and conclude that they want to reclaim the energy and vigor of their youth. They want to live longer, stay healthy, and enjoy a high quality of life. At the same time, they find themselves putting on a few pounds and experiencing unwelcome aches and pains.

What should we do, slow down and smell the roses or pump up our activity levels? The answer is clear. No matter our age, we can improve almost every facet of our physical, emotional, and mental health through a regular exercise program. More than two-thirds of Americans age 50 to 79 agree that exercise is the best thing for health. The reasons given for exercising, in order of priority, were to prevent disease, reduce stress, and fight the aging process (Milner 2002).

So why don't people get off the couch and get active? Some typical excuses are "I just don't have time to fit in exercise," "I don't have a tennis partner or regular game," "My tennis skills are not very good," "Going to the gym is boring, more like work than play," "I can't afford it," and "My body just can't stand the strain of sports any longer. It even hurts to get out of bed in the morning."

Most people say that if they knew how to go about a sensible activity program that they would enjoy, they would do it, but they just don't know how. Throughout this book, we'll offer solutions, advice, and instruction to eliminate any excuses you may have.

Anecdotal evidence and our personal experience lead us to conclude that most people are looking for similar things from the sport of tennis:

- Partners and opponents who are fun to be around and share similar expectations about their tennis
- Interaction with groups of other people, whether in a learning, competitive, or social situation

Who wants to be a couch potato?

© 2008 Ben Boyd

- An even balance between the challenge of competition and personal skill in the sport
- A healthy, vigorous activity that seems like play rather than work
- A tennis facility that offers a pleasant, safe, clean, and comfortable environment
- Tennis staff and teaching professionals who are friendly and organized, are good at matching players with partners and opponents, and are energetic

What are your expectations for tennis? Are you looking primarily for a good, physical workout? Or perhaps the challenge of learning and refining tennis skills? Maybe you revel in competition at any level and love to test yourself in situations where performance counts. Some of you just enjoy spending time with your spouse or other family members and seek an active way to do that. Most people over 50 value spending time with friends and making new friends, so the social time after play or spontaneous social plans that evolve may be a bonus. Once you clarify your expectations for tennis play, you can begin to make smart decisions about where to play and how to maximize the opportunities that are offered.

Find a Facility

Visit several tennis facilities, both public and private, to try them out. Keeping your financial situation in mind, join a facility where the people you meet fit what you're looking for. Notice whether players socialize after play, whether refreshments are offered on the spot, and whether the facility itself appeals to you. Depending on your personal needs, you might be happiest playing at a public park, local high school, or a public or private club. Services tend to be better at facilities where you have to pay a bit more, but that is a personal decision.

Ask people who have played at the facility for some time if they enjoy the people and benefit from the professional staff. Not many people leave a tennis facility because they had too many friends there or the staff just seemed too happy, friendly, and accommodating.

Check out the tennis programs offered for different ages and abilities. Are a newsletter, bulletin board, and e-mail contact for members available? Are other amenities offered such as swimming, refreshments, strength training, massage therapists, and a pro shop with equipment and restringing services? Social events off the tennis court indicate that members also enjoy spending time together. Find out how to reserve a court and the availability at times when you want to play.

Tennis is a social sport, too.

Choose a Type of Court

Choosing a facility based on the type of tennis courts it offers may seem to be an insignificant detail, but it can be a key ingredient in protecting your health for the future. Softer courts made of clay or a composition material such as Har-Tru are the most forgiving. Because of the softer surface, they are easier on the joints and back during play and reduce the aches and pains players may feel the day after playing.

Although clay courts are most popular on the East Coast of the United States, more are being built west of the Mississippi River because of advances in technology and underground watering systems that can be used where water is limited. The underground systems use less water and lose almost none to evaporation because the water comes upward from the bottom surface of the court.

Another advantage of clay courts is that the speed of play is noticeably slower than on most hard courts. That difference gives you more time to reach the ball and prepare for a shot. It also keeps the ball in play longer and makes for more interesting games strategically.

Many public facilities do not have clay courts because of the expense of upkeep and watering, although in Florida they are plentiful. Colleges, universities, and public high schools almost always choose hard surfaces because of limited budgets for maintenance.

Advances in hard-court technology have improved the options for hard-court tennis. Tennis court builders now offer cushioned surfaces of various thicknesses that provide a cushion beneath the harder court surface. They also can apply the top surface in a way that slows the ball after the bounce, thus increasing the length of rallies just like clay courts do. Choose a cushioned hard court if you have an option. Clay courts are better if they are available in your area. Once you grow accustomed to playing on softer, slower courts, you will never be happy with hard courts again.

Learn From a Professional

Tennis teaching professionals are in the service industry and they understand that their job is to satisfy customers and create an environment in which you can fulfill your personal tennis expectations. If you think of tennis pros as people who only give lessons to improve tennis technique, you are overlooking some of their most important duties in serving customers.

An effective tennis professional listens to your expectations and tries to guide you into groups of players who share similar interests. Ask for help finding hitting partners, competitive programs within the facility, and competitive teams that play teams from other facilities. Is there a facility ladder or tournament? What about group lessons? Are they strategic or stroke oriented?

Successful teaching professionals will often offer to hit with you briefly, size up your skills and abilities, and match you with compatible partners. They will also offer e-mail addresses and telephone numbers for prospective playing partners.

Check out the certification and experience of the tennis teaching staff at any facility you are considering. At a minimum, teaching professionals should be certified by the United States Professional Tennis Association (USPTA) or the Professional Tennis Registry (PTR). Whether you take regular lessons or not, the pro is your key ally in recommending programs, matching playing partners, and being your overall tennis resource.

If you are new to tennis or returning to the game, group instruction or drills are the key. Group instruction is more fun and more affordable than individual lessons. Plus, you'll get to meet other players at your level who can become playing partners. A skilled teaching professional usually works with groups up to six per court for instruction, thus cutting your costs

Group lessons just make good "cents."

significantly. Be sure to ask whether the group instruction is aimed at strategic or technique work or a combination of both.

You may be thinking that you'd rather work on your tennis game on your own rather than pay someone for help. Learning tennis on your own is usually inefficient, ineffective, and fraught with pitfalls. Teaching yourself is simply a matter of trial-and-error learning, which is slow, tedious, and generally counterproductive. Even though you practice hard, you may simply be repeating poor technique and bad habits. Let a teaching professional transfer his or her knowledge and experience to you and enhance your learning curve significantly.

If you have a special problem or need emergency first aid for a recalcitrant tennis stroke, consider a half-hour or an hour-long private lesson. Make sure the teaching professional understands your expectations for the lesson. If you've suffered from an injury, chances are your technique could be adjusted to prevent further recurrences. If your physical limitations have become a recurring liability, a teaching pro can suggest ways to compensate that may never have occurred to you. For example, a rotator cuff injury may hamper the power of your serve, but you could switch to an emphasis on placement, variety, and depth with guidance from the pro on how to do that.

Choosing the teaching professional who is right for you may happen accidentally, but just like when engaging other professionals, it helps to know what qualities you are looking for. Like all of us, teaching professionals vary in their approach, personality, and preferences. If you are lucky enough to have several choices of teaching professionals at one facility, you might try out more than one to judge your preference. Once you begin to work with one professional, stick with him or her for a while. Players who go from one to another generally succeed in confusing themselves and the pros, too.

If you choose a tennis facility that is open to the public, such as courts located at a public high school, you probably won't have the services of a teaching professional at that site. However, it is often the case on public courts that some type of instruction is offered through a community tennis program, normally during the summer. You also should not rule out seeking help from a teaching pro at a local facility who is allowed to teach people who are not regular members. Many commercial public facilities have a teaching professional, and some tennis clubs allow their staff to teach outside guests with the hope that a guest is a prospective member.

Engage in Competition

Regularly scheduled round-robin play and in-house leagues are great ways to ensure moderately competitive play at your home facility. These provide built-in partners, and you don't have to arrange games yourself. Many facilities also offer a challenge ladder for people to challenge others and arrange a time to play that is mutually convenient.

If you're a bit more competitive, check out the teams that play in local interfacility leagues and the Unites States Tennis Association (USTA) leagues. You'll be pleased to know that USTA offers singles, doubles, and mixed competition for people 50 and over at various skill levels that ensures fair and balanced competition.

Develop a 50-Plus Tennis Game

If you've always thought of player development as something reserved for young, promising players, let us change your mind. All players are in the process of developing their tennis games. And at this stage of life, you will need to adjust to physical realities and realize new benefits.

For most players over 50, doubles becomes the game of choice. In doubles, each player has less of the court to cover. Also it's more fun

Fun, friends, and fitness in tennis!

to share the experience with a partner, and the situations that occur in doubles produce some amazing points that get better with retelling after the match. Even so, some players still enjoy the game of singles and revel in the uniqueness of the game.

After 50, the old zip on shots just isn't there. To adjust, you need to focus on strategy, consistency, and placement to win points. The old explosiveness to get to the ball is replaced by smart anticipation of the opponent's shot. You'll need to learn to cover the court with less movement and rely more on anticipating your opponent's possible shots. Jumping to smash an opponent's lob for a winner is replaced by learning to play a bit farther back from the net and anticipate when the lob is coming. Because service aces are few and far between, depth, spin, placement, and disguise become critical on the serve. Retreating is more difficult than moving forward, so learning to play more balls out of the air, even from midcourt, becomes a necessary skill. An area you may have heard referred to as *no man's land* often becomes your home base by choice to prevent having to backpedal in a panic situation.

Many opponents at this age are wily competitors who are unlikely to beat themselves. You need to outthink them because you can't just hit them off the court. The coming chapters offer specific advice on how to make these changes to your game. Naturally, our focus will begin with doubles because that is the game of choice for most seniors, although we will explore the singles game in chapters 8 and 9.

WORDS TO THE WISE

- Plan to play tennis at least through your 80s.
- Decide what you expect from tennis and try to strike the right balance between regular play, fun, social activity, instruction, and competition.
- Find a tennis facility in which you feel comfortable and where the people are friendly.
- Enlist the help of a tennis teaching professional to find compatible players, program choices, and competitive opportunities and to help you improve strategy or technique.
- Begin your personal process of player development by learning how to play tennis after age 50. Pay special attention to the advice in the coming chapters on both doubles and singles play for changes you might consider as you age.

CHAPTER

2

Tennis Is a Physical Game

The game of tennis can be both an aerobic and anaerobic physical activity. Aerobic simply means the body is working with oxygen to produce energy. A typical match can range from an hour to up to three hours, demanding an efficient blood supply to carry oxygen from the heart to the working muscles. The aerobic benefits of tennis are heightened when you play an evenly contested match in which the ball stays in play for multiple shots during each point. There is not much aerobic benefit to tennis if a match consists of error followed by error followed by retrieving balls. Tennis typically taps into the aerobic system for about 10 to 20 percent of energy needs during a match, but the aerobic system does provide an essential endurance component over the length of a long match or multiple matches played in succession. Recreational tennis players who play a moderately active, friendly game of doubles often tap into their aerobic energy systems more than those who play at a more intense competitive level.

The anaerobic benefits of tennis come from shorter periods of intense physical activity, bursts of sprinting to reach the ball followed by short periods of rest between points. Slightly longer rest periods are allowed at the changeover of ends of the court after odd-numbered games. This type of activity, sometimes called interval training, is one of the most

© Associated Press

Bjorn Borg wins the 1980 French Open. Even winning the French Open six times didn't raise his pulse.

efficient ways to achieve a high-quality workout. It is marked by intense periods of activity interspersed with short periods of less intensity that allow for recovery. Competitive tennis at higher skill levels relies on the anaerobic system to provide up to 70 percent of the energy used in a match.

One of the most reliable measures of exercise intensity is to monitor your heart rate during activity. Finely tuned athletes tend to have lower heart rates than average people and recover more quickly from exertion to their normal resting heart rate. Bjorn Borg, the stoic Swede who won Wimbledon five times and the French Open six times, was reported to have a resting heart rate of 45 beats per minute, compared to an average heart rate of 70 to 76 beats per minute. We don't know if tennis caused that low rate, but we do know that playing tennis is good for your heart. In fact, the Cleveland Clinic Heart Center, ranked number one in the United States for 10 years in row, says that three hours of moderate aerobic exercise every week can cut the risk of developing heart disease by 50 percent (Blackburn 2001).

Exercise helps reduce blood pressure, relieves stress, and burns calories. All of these play a vital role in reducing the risk of heart disease, the number one killing disease among both men and women. But tennis offers more. Regular tennis play also improves overall physical coordination, dynamic balance, and eye–hand coordination. Twisting and turning during tennis play help develop overall flexibility, body control, and bone density. Each of these benefits are critical as we age because we tend to lose aerobic and anaerobic capacity, flexibility, bone density, and muscular strength and endurance directly as a result of the aging process. The good news is that through regular physical activity, we can slow the decline in our physical capabilities dramatically until well into our eighth decade. Let's take a look at how to get the most physical benefit out of playing tennis.

Sustain a Tennis Rally

Rallying the tennis ball is the key to great physical activity and aerobic exercise. In a *rally,* players keep the ball in play with exchanges that last three, four, or more hits on every point. Keep a few extra tennis balls in your pocket so that you can immediately put another ball in play after an error by either player.

If you venture onto the court to hit with a partner who bashes the ball around the court with little regard for control, placement, or consistency, the physical benefits of playing tennis will be minimal. In fact, you'll spend a lot of the time walking to retrieve errant shots and bending over to pick them up—not our idea of fun. Good rally partners can be friends or acquaintances of either gender, spouses, grandkids, or the club champion. Just be sure the goal is clear—keep the ball in play and maximize physical activity.

If you want some excellent exercise, learn to rally consistently with a partner. You'll make more friends, perspire a little, raise your heart rate into a training zone, and have fun, too. The following are tips for consistency during a rally.

Partners start close to the net, rallying the ball back and forth gently in the service boxes. Move your opponent from side to side. Keep your backswing short (less than half the length of a normal backswing) because you don't need power, and you have no time for a longer swing.

With both players at the baseline, focus on consistency by aiming 3 to 5 feet (1 to 1.5 meters) over the net on every shot and hitting moderately paced shots. (If your shot hits the net, open your racket face a bit more.) From the baseline, use a full backswing to drive the ball over the net. Begin the

Rallying on the shorter court promotes timing and touch.

forward swing below the ball, contact the ball at waist height, and finish with the racket above your opposite shoulder. If you use just half of the court, from the centerline to the doubles sideline for instance, shots will be easy to reach and fewer errors are likely.

To practice consistency, use only half the court.

STROKE DOCTOR

Check to see if you are moving into position quickly enough to be in balance before you swing. To improve timing, say to yourself "bounce" as the ball bounces and "hit" as you contact the ball. Try to contact the ball in your strike zone about waist high on every shot. Your arm should be comfortably extended but not locked at the elbow when you contact the ball.

Once your exchanges consistently comprise more than five hits, expand your hitting area to the entire singles court. Move your partner from side to side by using the racket face at the contact point to control the direction of the shot. The key to controlling the direction of any shot is to face the racket strings toward the intended target at the point of contact. After a few minutes, one player hits all shots crosscourt and the other hits down the line. You'll find out quickly who does all the running and why the crosscourt shot is the best choice most of the time.

To improve the depth of your shots, agree that every ball must land behind the service line or the rally stops. Aim your shots higher over the net to add depth. If you want a good workout, move each other up and back as well as side to side. Think of the court as four quadrants. Your goal is to place a shot in various quadrants during a rally. Now watch your opponent run.

Keep score. Whether you think you are competitive or not, keeping score makes you accountable, allows you to set a goal, and improves concentration. You win a point every time your opponent misses during any of the rally exercises.

Vary the activity by having one player at the net and one at the baseline. Start by keeping the ball in play for several shots (maybe three or four) and then allow either player to end the point. Use half of the court on one side to restrict the area and encourage consistency. After a while, add the variation of both players hitting crosscourt.

There you have it—a tennis rally that provides great physical activity. As you improve your consistency and accuracy, you'll have more tennis friends to play with. Players of different ability levels can still have fun rallying because the goal is activity. If you want to challenge the better player, use a handicap system such as restricting the better player to certain shots or hitting only to certain areas of the court. For example, the better player has to hit every ball into the deep, right quadrant of the court while his or her hitting partner is free to aim anywhere in the singles court.

If you have a rally session for half an hour every other day, you could burn several hundred calories, have fun, and maybe reduce your resting heart rate. Your tennis skills will improve quickly, too.

Try Cardio Tennis

Here's a different idea to get the full benefit of tennis for your cardiorespiratory system. Try Cardio Tennis, a fun group activity featuring tennis drills that give players of all abilities an ultimate, high-energy workout. Led by a tennis teaching professional, Cardio Tennis includes a warm-up, cardio workout, and cool-down—all in an hour. It's perfect for an early morning, lunchtime, or after-work energizer.

During the hour, you'll elevate your heart rate into your aerobic training zone. To find your aerobic training zone, subtract your age from the number 220. Multiply that number by 65 percent (0.65) to 85 percent (0.85), depending on how hard you want to train. For example, let's say Harry is 58 years old and new to Cardio Tennis. He should probably start by training at 65 percent of his maximum heart rate: $220 - 58 = 162 \times 0.65 = 105$ beats per minute.

Cardio Tennis will get your heart pumping.

The best way to monitor your heart rate is by using a heart rate monitor, but don't worry if one isn't available. You can take your pulse the old-fashioned way at your neck or wrist.

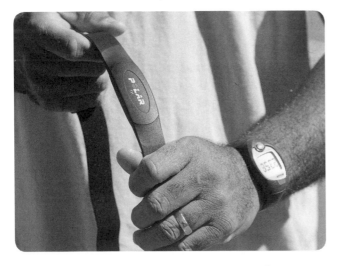

Use a heart rate monitor to measure exercise intensity.

During the activity session, a teaching pro feeds tennis balls all over the court to the group of players. Music in the background can raise energy levels, and the group spirit will do the rest. It's a great activity, and you'll get to hit lots of tennis balls. For information on a Cardio Tennis program near you, visit www.cardiotennis. com or check with your local tennis facility for programs.

Use Tennis for Weight Control

If you keep up on the health of Americans, you know there is a growing epidemic of overweight and obesity. Even if you'd just like to lose a few pounds in the right places to look the age you feel, tennis can be the golden cure.

Weight control is simply a matter of balancing the amount and type of food you take into the body with caloric expenditure. As you age, body metabolism slows and calories tend to be absorbed and stored rather than expended. Raising metabolism through physical activity can help you burn more calories, even at rest, and is especially important as you age.

A 135-pound (61.2-kilogram) woman who plays one hour of singles tennis can burn 420 calories. She would burn about 330 calories playing doubles. An average-size man will burn about 600 calories playing singles and 425 calories playing doubles. A woman who plays three times a week for an hour and half will burn a minimum of 1,500 calories per week; a man would burn closer to 2,000 calories per week.

© 2008 Ben Boyd

Tennis helps players look and feel fit.

You should also know that the number of calories burned is directly related to how physically active your play is. When you play with evenly matched opponents, keep the ball in play for several exchanges on each point, and use the whole court for placement of shots, the energy expenditure goes up significantly. To maximize the value of tennis for weight control, eat a healthy, balanced diet; control food portion sizes; exercise regularly; and supplement tennis with other physical activities.

Include Supplementary Physical Activities

Tennis is not the perfect physical activity, but it is close. It combines many physical benefits and challenges players physically in ways that make them healthier, stronger, and fitter. As the motto of the Olympic Games says, "Citius, Altius, Fortius," which means "faster, higher, and stronger."

But to really take care of your body after age 50, you may need to add other physical activities to your weekly regimen as a complement to tennis. We'll cover some ideas in more detail in later chapters, but for now, think about learning how to warm up and cool down correctly to increase flexibility and prevent injuries. (Chapter 11 provides more information on specific complementary physical activities for tennis players.)

Strength training is also a must, beginning with key postural muscles and working toward the extremities. Strengthening your muscles will increase the efficiency of your tennis skills and help prevent injuries. Because aging naturally reduces muscular strength, training muscles by overloading them off the tennis court is critical to maintaining overall muscular strength and endurance. You can use your body weight, resistance bands, exercise balls, free weights, or machines, but the bottom line is that you have to overload your muscles to increase strength and endurance. Plan on 30 minutes of strength and flexibility training three times a week to train for tennis play. It's a great investment. If you adopt a simple regimen of strength and flexibility training to complement your tennis, you will hit the gold standard for taking care of your body.

Overall physical fitness is composed of four main components: cardiorespiratory fitness, flexibility, muscular strength and endurance, and body composition (ratio of muscle to fat). Tennis can take care of cardiorespiratory and body composition needs. Tennis helps to develop flexibility and muscular strength, but it needs some assistance off the tennis court as well. That's all we're saying!

Resistance bands are an easy way to overload muscles and build strength.

WORDS TO THE WISE

- Tennis is a terrific physical activity.
- Learning to rally well is good for your heart, and you'll make lots of friends.
- Cardio Tennis is a blast!
- You don't see many overweight tennis players.
- Do yourself a favor by supplementing your tennis with flexibility and strength training along with proper warm-up and cool-down regimens (see chapter 11).

Learning to Love Competition

In chapter 2, we looked at the physical benefits of tennis and how you can use tennis to boost your physical fitness. Now it's time to consider the psychological challenges and benefits of tennis, especially during competitive play.

At its core, the sport of tennis is a contest between two or four competitors who try to hit the ball over the net and within the court boundaries one more time than their opponents. Success results in earning a point for a ball that is not successfully returned.

Some tennis players, perhaps you are among them, shy away from the competitive aspect of tennis because it takes away the fun of the game by adding pressure to succeed based on racket skill. Perhaps you avoid competition because you enjoy physical activities that are less stressful and place more emphasis on participating than on competing. Even if this describes your attitude, adding competitive elements to your tennis can enhance your motivation to play. We urge you to consider trying to play competitive tennis at a level that is comfortable and challenges your execution of skill and strategy against a variety of opponents. If you follow the advice offered in this chapter, you may find that competition becomes fun if you have the right attitude and the emotional and psychological skills to deal with the perceived pressure of keeping score.

Most people would say they play tennis, or any sport, for fun. But if you watch them play, it may seem like anything but fun. If you've thought that sports are more like work than fun, perhaps the information in this chapter will alter your attitude, and you will learn to love competition.

Psychologists have suggested that fun occurs when there is an even balance between the overall skill of the performer and the challenge presented by the sport (Danish 1990). If the challenge of the sport is too great, an athlete becomes frustrated. If the challenge is too easy, boredom sets in. The trick then is to find a level of tennis competition that is suitable for your skill and competitive level. This does not mean playing with the same partners and opponents all the time, otherwise boredom will eventually occur. Seek multiple partners and opponents at appropriate levels and enjoy every playing experience.

Remember to *play* tennis. The word play conjures up a childlike quality of enjoyment, delight, and excitement. Remember when you couldn't wait to go out to play? Forget about working out or stressing out—just play for the fun of it.

© 2008 Ben Boyd

Imagine how the racket feels about the player.

Enjoying Competition

Competitive tennis is simply a way of testing your skill and tracking your performance by keeping score. Although you could do that simply by counting the number of successful shots in a rally with a cooperative practice partner, it is quite another task if the person or people on the other side of the net don't cooperate. Your goal for competitive tennis is to perform as well as you can in spite of the difficulty of the tasks that your opponents present to you. Competition in life can bring out the best in us or the worst. Success is complicated and the score does not always indicate the quality of performance.

Tennis players sometimes earn a label as a winner or a loser. The fact is those labels are unreliable descriptions of any player in competitive sport. After all, you may win consistently against players of inferior skill or lose often to better players. The play of your opponent is out of your control. On any given day, half of those who play tennis will win and half will lose. Your odds are only 50-50 if you are playing against opponents of equal ability.

The score does not always indicate the quality of performance.

A better way to evaluate success in tennis is to judge your performance against your own standard. In fact, we suggest that your goal in competitive tennis should be to play as well as you can, with full effort, on any given day. Great athletes have figured out that their goal in competition should be to perform as well as they can and let the outcome take care of itself:

> *Andre Agassi:* "For me, the goal is to see if I can play better today than I did yesterday."
>
> *Billie Jean King:* "When you stay in the process is when you win. Not when you get into the end results."

You won't hear Tiger Woods setting the goal of winning a tournament. Instead he consistently focuses on his own performance and playing to the best of his ability (Saviano 2003). Playing well means giving full effort to your performance using your tennis skills, strategy, and tactics and controlling your mind and emotions. Some days you will play great and other days not so well. The key question is whether you exerted a full and complete effort that day and did the best you could. If the answer is yes, you achieved your goal.

There are many barriers that might keep you from enjoying competition or from playing your best. For example, your mind and emotions have a huge impact on your competitive performance. The following sections explore techniques for controlling your mind and emotions; setting performance rather than outcome goals; keeping score; using positive self-talk; combating anxiety, nerves, and choking; practicing with pressure; improving focus and concentration; analyzing play after the match; and winning versus success (playing for fun).

Controlling Your Mind and Emotions

At every level of play, thoughts and feelings affect tennis performance. Players at lower skill levels have to think about every shot just to execute it. At higher skill levels, skills and even strategy become almost automatic, but emotions may become the one factor that determines how well a player performs on a given day.

Numerous books have been written about how to achieve mental toughness, but that just might miss the point. For competition, it may be more important to learn emotional toughness. Emotions provide the energy that allows us to perform well. However, it does not follow that more energy will necessarily produce a great performance. Your best performance will occur when you reach the optimal level of arousal to perform a task. Finding your optimal arousal level and keeping it throughout a match is the key to performing well. Most players find their optimal arousal level quite by accident through trial and error. They report that they feel focused, hopeful, challenged, and energized with high positive energy. Once you've experienced these feelings during play, you need to identify what produced them and try to recreate them on demand.

If your emotional arousal level is too low, your performance will suffer from lack of energy and unfocused or lethargic play. Raise your arousal level before a match by exercising vigorously in the warm-up, by giving yourself a pep talk, by listening to high-energy music, or by discussing your game plan with your partner. If you find your arousal level sinking during a match, it may be helpful to refocus your attention on your game plan and strategy. You should also raise your energy level by hustling after every ball and getting into an optimal hitting position as quickly as you can.

Music and exercise can help raise your arousal level.

At the opposite extreme, if emotional arousal is too high, you may become anxious, nervous, erratic, and tense. For most people who play tennis competitively, just worrying about winning and losing can raise their arousal level too high.

Anxiety is often described as worry and tension and being upset or distracted. Typically, anxiety creates physical symptoms such as cold hands, muscle tension, hyperventilation, and a queasy feeling in the stomach (butterflies). Anxiety of this type is often relieved by relaxing music, massage, a hot shower, or routines such as deep breathing and alternately tensing and relaxing muscle groups. During a match, be sure to take your time between points, relax your muscles, and breathe deeply. You can also shove anxiety away by focusing clearly on your game plan and resolving to execute it regardless of the score.

The mind can also be the site of anxiety in the form of worry, loss of focus, racing thoughts, or dwelling on past competitive failures. The best antidote for the mental symptoms of anxiety is to distract yourself with thoughts unrelated to tennis, review your performance goals, or use imagery techniques to refocus your thoughts. Use the time during the changeover of sides to relax, refocus, and imagine yourself executing the shot patterns you believe will be successful against your opponent. Use positive imagery by picturing in your mind's eye how you will look performing at your best.

As you gain competitive experience, begin to note how you feel when you play your best tennis. After the match, write down how you felt and what your prematch routine was that day. If you can recapture that feeling every time you play, your performances will improve. On those days when your emotions are getting the best of you, recall a good match in your past and remember how you felt. Review your match preparation and resolve before your next match to warm up and stretch properly, groove your shots the day before, or perhaps play a few games before the match on game day to reduce nervousness. Once you find a formula for match preparation that works, stick with it.

Setting Performance Goals

The only thing you can control in competition is your effort toward a goal. You cannot control your opponents' play, the conditions, the audience, line calls, bad bounces, or luck. In doubles, you have to accept that you also can't control your partner's play. You can't even control your own quality of play, just the effort you put toward it.

Many people set *outcome goals* before a match:

- I just want to win this match.
- Winning this match will put us in the finals.
- We want revenge for losing to these guys last week.
- Let's win in straight sets.
- We can't lose to these kids.

We suggest that you discard that type of goal and develop specific *performance goals* for each match, such as the following:

- I'm going to get at least 50 percent of my first serves in.
- On every short ball, I'm going to hit an approach shot and join my partner at the net.
- At the net, I'm going to poach at least once each game.
- I will take my time before serving and during the changeover after odd games.
- I'm going to hustle with full effort to every ball so that I am set up in a balanced position and ready to swing before the ball arrives.
- I will hit high-percentage shots while returning serve and put the pressure on the serving team.

As you play with performance goals, you'll find that the quality of your game typically improves and your chance of a favorable outcome is greatly enhanced. You may not win the match, but you will have the satisfaction of doing the best you could for that day.

Keeping Score

If you're new to the game, you may think tennis scoring is confusing. Although tennis scoring is not logical, it's pretty easy to get the hang of it. The first point of a game earns a score of 15 for that player. If he also wins the second point, his score is 30. A third point earns a score of 40, and a fourth point results in his winning the game, unless both players have won three point (score is tied at 40, or deuce). In that situation, the next player to win a point earns advantage, and if he wins the next point, he wins the game. If his opponent wins the next point, the score goes back to deuce.

To win a set, a player must win at least six games and be ahead by two games. Most competitive matches are the best two out of three sets to determine the winner. If a set score becomes tied at 6-6, usually players play a tiebreak. During a tiebreak, players try to earn the best of 12 points (must win by 2) to determine the winner of the set.

It is astounding the number of matches in which a dispute arises over the score. Part of being a good competitor is to know the score of the game and set so you can make a wise decision about the way to play the next point. Some players like to gamble more than others do, and players who gamble with poor-percentage shots better know the score.

Suppose you have a 25 percent chance of hitting a service ace, but if you miss, your opponent will likely pound your feeble second serve. When should you go for an ace: early in a game, in a tiebreak, at match point, early in a set, on a break point against you, or anytime? Although early in a game and early in a set are acceptable answers, a better answer is to improve your second serve. Discuss with your partner when to take more risks and when to play safer shots. Once you decide, you can both anticipate the type of point that is likely to occur and be in the best position. If you have opposing tactics in mind, there is sure to be confusion, frustration, and unpleasant surprises.

Here is the best plan for keeping score. If the courts have score markers, make sure you change them as you change sides of the net and confirm the score with your opponents. During each game, the server should call the score before the serve loudly enough for all players to hear. The Code of Tennis is a supplement to the Rules of Tennis for players in unofficiated matches. It states, "The server shall announce the score before each point" (USTA 2000). If there is a question about the score, settle it immediately to avoid a dispute later on.

If your opponents do not call the score, there is nothing to prevent the receiving team from doing so, and after a while they will probably get the idea. Nothing is more upsetting than a silly scoring dispute that could have been avoided. If you don't expect to play with an umpire present, plan to call the score to keep your friends and protect yourself against others.

You've probably heard players refer to key points that occur during a match. Even professional players and coaches mention that one player played the so-called big points better than the opponent. Some books will advise you that the first point of a game, the 15-30 point, or lost set points are the most important. We've always heard that the seventh game in a set is crucial, as well.

We'd like to offer another way to look at the significance of each point. There are no key points in tennis. Each point counts just one, and over the course of a match, the player who wins the most overall points will win nearly every time. The best competitors play every point to the best of their ability.

Have you ever played or watched a match where one player had a large lead, perhaps even 5-0 in a set, and lost the set. Can you identify the key point in that set? How about players who are down 6-2, 4-1 and come back to win. It happens more than you might think.

If you lose what you consider to be a key point, does that mean you will lose the set or match? Should you just give up competing at that point? Clearly the answer is no, unless it is the last point. We can guarantee that if you think about certain points as key, you'll become more anxious and play the point poorly. Forget about losing key points and keep playing as smart and as hard as you can until the match is over.

We have to add one caveat about certain points, though. You do have a choice in the amount of risk to take for any point throughout the match. When the score tells you a game, set, or match hangs in the balance, smart competitors choose the highest-percentage shots and shift the pressure back to their opponents.

Controlling Your Mind Through Positive Self-Talk

When you walk past a row of tennis courts, you're likely to overhear players make comments to themselves such as these:

- What an idiot!
- I can't believe I just missed that shot.
- Watch the ball!

- Move your feet, stupid.
- What a bad bounce or lucky net cord.

You might also hear profanity. And those are just the comments that are audible. There are probably worse comments that are unspoken. These are examples of negative self-talk, which is a quick trip to a loss of confidence. Talk to yourself the way you'd like to be treated by your best friend. Thoughts and comments should be positive, optimistic, and specific. Here are better examples of self-talk:

- I'll get the next one; this match isn't over yet.
- Next time, I'll prepare earlier for the shot.
- Play the percentages next time.
- Take your time and relax.
- Good effort, just bad luck.

Also use these same types of comments with your partner if you want to encourage him after an error. Positive and optimistic are the keys.

Combating Nerves, Anxiety, and Choking

It has happened before. During a tiebreak in the third set with her team up 6-5, all Connie had to do was get her serve in to put her team in good position to win. Alas, her powerful first serve went out, and her meager attempt at a second serve landed in the net. Faced with a score of 6-6, Connie was completely unnerved and double-faulted again to put her team behind 6-7. Would you say she choked during this tiebreak? Has something similar happened to you? Could it have been prevented?

Our answers are yes, she probably choked, it has happened to us, and we know that you can reduce the chances of a repeat performance, but we can't guarantee it. Even the very best athletes in the world choke or are the victims of nerves, anxiety, or the pressure of the moment. Over thousands of tennis matches, we've watched our favorite professional players fail. Pete Sampras admitted to nervousness; so did Andre Agassi. We even watched Rod Laver double-fault in a fifth-set tiebreak against Ken Rosewall in the World Championship Tournament finals in 1972. (Laver is one of the greatest, if not the best, player of all time!) Martina Navratilova, Chris Evert, Jennifer Capriati, Steffi Graf, Lindsay Davenport, and countless others have been a victim of their nerves a few times.

The difference between these great players and most of us is that they rarely choke; their tolerance to pressure is quite high, and they have a plan to deal with it. But if the pressure becomes too great, they are susceptible to nerves just like we are.

Typical responses to anxiety about the outcome of a match include rushing between points and games and during shots; not moving into position (feet of lead); tension and tightness in the upper body (steel elbow); short, shallow breathing and racing heartbeat; loss of focus; and hitting too hard or hitting too soft. We all know the signs. The question is, is there anything we can do to change these feelings? Here are few strategies to try:

- As tension mounts during a match, slow down and take your time. Rushing between serves is a dead giveaway that nerves are getting the better of you. Mentally rehearse your performance goals, and plan how to play the next shot or point.

- As the point begins, get on your toes and move quickly into position. Even if your feet feel like lead weights, shake it off and get to the ball early.

- Between points, take a couple of deep, slow breaths and smile. After all, if you weren't a pretty good competitor, you wouldn't even be in a tight match.

- Relax your upper body by alternately tightening and relaxing the muscles in your chest, back, shoulders, arms, and hands. Help fight an elbow that feels like it is made of steel by lengthening your follow-through on every shot.

- Act as if you are confident, under control, and feeling good. As you act a certain way, your body takes its cues from your behavior. If your shoulders are slumped and head is down and you wear a frown on your face, you will only sink deeper into an emotionally depressed mood.

- Focus your attention on the next point, forget past points, and don't be tempted by the future. The only point that matters is the next one you play.

- Play the ball at about 75 percent of your maximum pace. This reduces risk without resorting to just pushing the ball around the court. Focus on early positioning, good follow-through on every shot, and choosing high-percentage shots.

Practicing With Pressure

Players who play well under pressure aren't born that way. They've developed pressure tolerance through practicing and playing with pressure and discovering techniques to combat anxiety. Most people don't practice pressure situations, so when they occur in competition, panic sets in. The following are ways to create pressure situations in practice so that you can develop your own coping strategy.

Pressure Serving and Receiving

Play a match with only one serve allowed per point. This will force you to get your first serve in and give you a true evaluation of just how dependable your serve really is. Or play a match with the rule that any missed return of serve results in the loss of the game no matter when it occurs. This rule cuts down the number of returns into the net.

By yourself, try to serve four consecutive serves in this order:

- Deuce court, to the outside half of box
- Deuce court, to the inside half of box
- Ad court, to the outside half of box
- Ad court, to the inside half of box

To increase the difficulty, the serve doesn't count unless it passes the baseline before the second bounce. That eliminates soft serves. Another way to add difficulty is to divide the service box into thirds. Instead of aiming for the outside half of the box, you reduce your target to the outside third of the box. You can also perform this drill in front of an audience of teammates or others. That will add more pressure for sure.

Scoring Adjustments

Simple scoring adjustments can add pressure by emphasizing a fewer number of points. This creates a similar situation to one you might face near the end of a competitive match when several hours of play might come down to a few well-played points. In the following situations, all other normal tennis rules apply; only the scoring technique is altered.

- Play the best three out of five, 12-point tiebreaks against another team.
- Play a 1-point tournament against several other teams. This is a single-elimination tournament with each round consisting of just 1 point. Let's say you start with eight teams. Each team draws a number. Teams 7 and 8 play the first round consisting of 1 point. The losing team is out, and the winner now plays the challenger, team 6. Play continues until only one team is left and is declared champions.
- Play a handicap system. The winner of the first game begins the second game down 1 point (love-15). If the set score goes to 2-0, the team

ahead is down 2 points. If the set score goes to 3-0, the leading team begins at love-40. This system works great for teams of different skill levels because it is difficult to start out a game down love-40 and still win. Sets and matches using this system tend to be very close.

Playing With an Audience

Did you ever notice that players who lack confidence always ask for a back court so no one can watch them? It's natural to hide when you believe you'll look foolish. To deal with the pressure of people watching, look for situations in which you can play on the first or show court. Random passersby will see you play a few points, and you will have an opportunity to adjust to their scrutiny. Ask teammates or friends to come watch you play and then learn to block out their presence until after the match.

Be inventive in designing your own ways to practice with pressure. Play on club ladders, local tournaments, round-robin events, mixed doubles, team matches, and anywhere someone is keeping score. As you gain confidence and skill, your pressure tolerance will increase.

Improving Concentration and Focus

Maintaining focus throughout a match is a critical battle for most tennis players. There are no timeouts or coaches allowed to help players refocus during a match, so it's up to you. We promise you will lose your concentration during every match. The more important fact is that you can regain it and sharpen your focus each time you play. The following are suggestions for improving your concentration.

You'll play your best tennis if you focus your attention on your performance goals, strategy, shot selection, shot execution, your racket, and the tennis ball. Your tennis performance will decrease if you focus attention on your opponent, the audience, key points, the possible outcome of the match, and previous points. Other hindrances to concentration include the sun, wind, noise, bad bounces, heat, cold, background, clothing, opponent's grunts, line calls, mannerisms, partner's play, and on and on.

To keep your concentration, change your object of focus. Focus your attention on the current point. Resist replaying past failures or imagining future points. Resolve to give full effort only to the point at hand. Control your eyes by looking at your court and your racket. Ignore distractions such as other matches, the elements, or spectators.

As you hit the ball, focus your full attention on the ball. Pick a spot on the ball to place the strings of your racket. Pay attention to your partner after every point by encouraging her, slapping high fives after a great point, or talking about a plan for the next point. Establish a routine during the changeover and stick to it. After a few seconds of relaxation, drinking, and toweling off, refocus on the match and upcoming game.

Expect your concentration to wander during a match. When that happens, accept it and use a cue word or phrase to reactivate your focus on the task at hand. Take a cue from your performance goals such as "let's get the ball in play on every service return."

Analyzing Play After the Match

After a match, spend a few minutes with your partner to assess your performance as a team and as individual players. This time is not well spent lamenting lost opportunities or outside factors that may have affected the outcome. Rather compare your team's performance and your play to the performance goals you set before the match. Be sure to analyze offensive and defensive strategy, shot selection, shot execution, and emotional control.

Although we do not advocate setting outcome goals for a match, the result does provide feedback on your performance. Just four match outcomes are possible:

• **You won and played well.** This is obviously the best result. You and your partner should pat yourselves on the back and enjoy a good performance. Later, after the celebration has passed, analyze the cause of your success so that you can repeat it in future matches.

• **You won but played poorly.** This result shows that either your opponents played poorly or were at a lower skill level. This situation can be dangerous and promote a false sense of security. Be specific in evaluating each part of your performance and determine how to improve or correct your play. Check to see if your effort and concentration were at optimal levels.

• **You lost but played well.** If the match was close and you played well as a team, you may have to accept that your opponents were better players, at least on that day. Search for positive feedback to give your partner, especially if the match was a close loss. See if you can pick one or two areas to improve as a team or an alternative tactic that could have changed the outcome.

• **You lost and played poorly.** With this result, it may be best to postpone the analysis if you are disappointed and emotionally upset. After a day or two, when your head has cleared, focus on one or two key areas and set performance goals for next time. Include an assessment of your prematch preparation routine and your emotional control during play.

Athletes are notorious for having selective memories after competition. However, there's a good reason for this: It is difficult to compete and also focus on retaining the information gathered during a match. You may want to enlist the help of a trusted coach, teammate, or spouse when evaluating a match. Their impressions are likely to be somewhat different from yours and not as likely to be colored by emotions. If certain performance problems persist, you may even consider asking an observer to chart specific results, such as the number of first serves you get in compared to double faults, times your team won points at the net, or the number of unforced errors. A simple numerical count of these statistics or others may provide valuable information that is quite different from what you remember.

Many athletes find excuses for poor performances in order to protect their egos. These excuses prevent them from concluding they just aren't very good competitors. Several problems occur if you rely on excuses to explain your performance in competition. Excuses are counterproductive to your mental and emotional control and they are typically used by low achievers. They are also tiresome and socially unacceptable. Most experienced tennis players view excuses as poor sporting behavior and eventually shy away from consistent excuse makers.

© 2008 Ben Boyd

A little wind should not be an excuse.

If you are looking for excuses, you can blame the court, racket, strings, wind, sun, spectators, opponents, lucky bounces, breaks, let cords, spin, noises, sweat, lights, heat, cold, muscle strain, headache, stomachache, dizziness, contact lenses, glasses, hat, sunscreen, jacket, split fingers, clay, blisters, shoes, other players, background, music, reflection, fences, lines, color of court, tennis balls, sports drink, snacks, birds, and fate. And the list goes on!

Psychologists state that high achievers attribute performance to things they can control such as effort, attitude, persistence, and their own performance. High achievers also choose competitive situations that are challenging and have unpredictable outcomes. Low achievers, on the other hand, tend to attribute performance to things outside their control such as luck, chance, or the play of opponents. They are often outcome oriented and tend to choose opponents who are overmatched or clearly superior in order to protect their egos.

Winning Versus Success

When the match is over, you've finished in either first or second place. Both places are admirable accomplishments, and even second place earns a silver medal. The only true losers are those who never play at all. Here is a final thought on loving competition, paraphrased from a famous quote from Teddy Roosevelt, 26th President of the United States:

Credit belongs not to critics nor couch potatoes, but to players who are actually on the tennis court, whose faces are marred by sweat and clay; who strive valiantly; who err and come up short again and again, because there is no effort without error and shortcoming; but who do actually strive to compete; who exhibit passion, commitment, and energy in a worthy contest; and in the best result, know the triumph of high achievement and who at the worst, if they fail, at least fail while daring greatly, so that their place shall never be with those cold, timid souls who neither know victory or defeat, or step foot on a tennis court.

WORDS TO THE WISE

- Have fun and remember to *play* tennis.
- Recognize that mental and emotional control skills are critical to competitive success.
- Learn to set performance goals and keep score throughout the match.
- Practice strategies to control your mind through self-talk.
- Practice strategies to control your emotions through deep breathing, muscle relaxation, slowing down between points, and aggressive movements during the point.
- Create pressure in practice and work on concentration skills.
- Analyze your play after the match.

Tuning in to Doubles

For most players over 50, doubles is the game. In fact, most adult recreational tennis players of all ages are hooked on doubles rather than singles play. The reasons are simple. Doubles play requires each player to cover a smaller section of the court. Instead of a 27-feet-wide (8.3-meters-wide) singles court, the doubles court is 36 feet (10.9 meters) wide and is covered by two players. The result is that the ball tends to be easier to reach and more balls stay in play.

Playing doubles maximizes court space. Where courts are in demand, doubles play allows twice as many people to play at one time. This is particularly true for indoor courts. Plus court expenses shared four ways are more economical than expenses shared by just two players.

Doubles is a more social game because it involves more people, and good teamwork can often overcome better-skilled opponents. The after-match relaxation time is often more fun, too, with four people offering their own special views of the match.

Most people enjoy the intellectual and strategic challenge of doubles, the wide variety of shots used, and the endless possibilities for exciting points. Doubles is similar to the game of chess, with its endless moves, countermoves, and variations; tennis singles more closely resembles the game of checkers, which is more simplistic and straightforward.

In the chapters that follow, we cover doubles strategy and tactics, technical racket skills and new skills that are essential to doubles play, advice on becoming a great partner and developing excellent teamwork, and advice on playing mixed doubles, even with your spouse.

The first chapter of part II, chapter 4, covers basic doubles strategy and tactics. Improving strategy and tactics is the fastest, most efficient way to learn to play better doubles. Once you understand the basic idea of a sport, it is a lot easier to see the importance of each shot and of court coverage. Plus, you'll realize why it's fun to improve the shots you have or add new ones.

Many players learn to play tennis by focusing on the execution of strokes. But often players with good stroke execution lose to players who appear to have worse strokes but just seem to win matches. The fact is, pretty tennis strokes don't necessarily produce good results unless they are applied to sound strategy or tactics.

Chapter 5 focuses on the advanced doubles strategy used by players at NTRP level 3.5 and above. If you are in this group, we suggest that you quickly review chapter 4 to refresh your understanding of the basics and then concentrate on the more advanced information in chapter 5. This chapter also contains practical adjustments for players over the age of 50.

Tennis skills are critical to executing strategy. In chapter 6, we assume you can execute fundamental tennis skills, such as serving, returning serve, and hitting ground strokes, volleys, and overhead shots. However, we also realize that you could probably use a few tips to improve these skills. In this chapter, we suggest a few ideas that have the potential to drastically improve performance. If you are still unhappy with your execution of certain shots, invest in a lesson with a certified teaching professional.

You may also want to add a few shots that are especially effective in doubles. Watch veteran players, ask their advice, and try to add a new shot every now and then. You should be able to hit both topspin and backspin, hard and soft, short and long, and high and low. Maybe you are comfortable from the backcourt but less so at the net. You like high volleys but not low ones. You feast off pace, but fall apart when your opponents only push every ball back. If you add just one new shot each year, by the time you're 75, you will be quite a player.

If you are a beginning player who lacks fundamental tennis skills, our recommendation is to join a group for basic instruction. After you've read chapter 4 and chapter 6, group instruction will be more meaningful and useful. Plus you'll be able to ask your teaching professional great questions during the group sessions.

In chapter 7 we focus on the agony and ecstasy of playing mixed doubles. You can broaden your circle of friends and your potential playing partners and opponents if you can play mixed doubles successfully. It takes special skills, flexible tactics, and good teamwork to play mixed doubles well. At the same time, one of the unique characteristics of tennis is the opportunity for players of both genders to compete with and against each other without special rules. Most sports simply can't boast that trait.

4

Fundamental Doubles Strategy and Tactics

All players will find this chapter a helpful review, although it will appeal particularly to players up to the National Tennis Rating Program (NTRP) level of 3.0. Whether you are just beginning to play tennis, returning to the sport, or continuing to play, if your skill level is 3.0 or lower, this chapter is critical.

Players at a skill level of 3.5 and higher may prefer to skim this chapter to refresh their knowledge of concepts already learned. Of particular interest will be the section on playing the middle of a point, because understanding those concepts is essential for gaining the most benefit from the next chapter. Chapter 5 is targeted to players at NTRP level 3.5 and above, but it assumes they understand the basic doubles strategy contained in this chapter.

Often the words *strategy* and *tactics* are used interchangeably as if there were no difference between them. But in tennis, there are subtle differences. Strategy is an overall game plan based on the principles of best-percentage tennis. Strategy is based on applying the laws of physics

Double your fun by playing doubles.

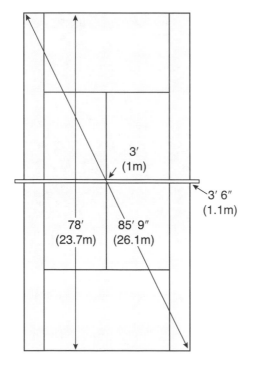

to sport. For example, hitting cross-court usually makes sense because the net is 6 inches (15 centimeters) lower in the middle than at the sides (figure 4.1), reducing your chance of error, and the distance of the court is longer on the diagonal than straight ahead—a distance of 85 feet, 9 inches (26.1 meters) versus 78 feet (23.7 meters) down the line. That's a 7-foot, 9-inch (2.4 meter) margin for error if you hit crosscourt, plus a lower net. So, whether you play singles or doubles, a crosscourt shot has a higher percentage of success than one hit straight ahead down the line.

Figure 4.1 Net height is 3 feet (1 meter) in the center but 3 feet, 6 inches (1.1 meter) at the side. A crosscourt shot has to travel 85 feet, 9 inches (26.1 meters), providing a good margin of error compared to a shot down the line, which travels only 78 feet (23.7 meters).

Because you have less court to cover in doubles than in singles (figure 4.2), the chances are more likely that both teams will reach more balls, and it may take longer to win the point unless you can reach the net position. If all four players in doubles played at the baseline, the points would likely last forever.

Tactics are an adjustment to overall strategy based on the game situation. If your opponents also know that strategically it is better to hit crosscourt, the net player in doubles may crowd the middle and attack your crosscourt shots. Your tactical response could be to hit down the sideline to the opening or to lob over the net player and eliminate the risk.

Another example of a tactical adjustment in doubles is to lob the ball to opponents on a particularly sunny or windy day. Normally, you would not want to give them a chance to hit an overhead smash, but with the complications of wind and sun, it might be a sound option.

Now that you understand the difference between strategy and tactics, you are ready to look at doubles play from that perspective. In addition, we present doubles strategy for playing a point. In coaching jargon, this is a game-based approach. It simply means we describe or illustrate a typical situation that occurs during a tennis point, suggest the strategic principles that apply, and ask you to apply them.

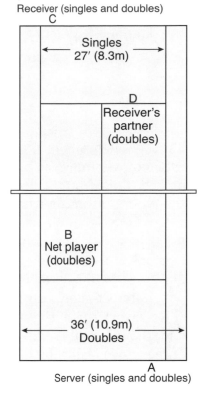

Figure 4.2 **In doubles, you have to defend about 18 feet (5.5 meters) in width, compared to 27 feet (8.3 meters) in singles.**

In many cases there is not one right answer, because the right answer depends on you, your partner, and your opponents. But we're convinced that if you understand the strategic principle and percentages of certain shots, you'll have a lot more fun.

At the risk of oversimplifying strategy for doubles play, here are the key topics we cover in this chapter:

- Positions on the court
- Bisecting the angle of possible returns
- Side-to-side movement as a team
- Beginning the point

- Playing the middle of a point
- Ending the point
- Basic team communication

Court Positions

Basic court positions (figure 4.3 shows positions before the serve) have evolved over the years based on individual player experiences. You don't have to follow our advice, but it sure makes a good starting point. We'll share our reasons for each position as we describe it.

Server: Normally, a player should serve from a position halfway between the center hash mark and the doubles sideline. This puts the server in the best position to play the return with the least amount of movement. Many players make the mistake of serving from a spot near the center hash mark, which immediately puts the server out of position for the next shot.

Receiver: This position is dictated by the server. The receiver should choose his lateral position by standing in the middle of the possible angles of the serve. Using the baseline as a guide, the receiver moves inside it if he expects a short serve and just behind it if the server places the ball deep in the service box with good pace.

Server's partner: The server's partner should imagine an X drawn in the service box and assume a position right smack in the middle. As the play begins, the server's partner needs to be ready to move sideways, up, or back, depending on the serve and return. At this level of play, many players stand quite close to the alley to guard it. However, this forces the server to cover three-fourths of the court while the server's partner just looks on.

Receiver's partner: The position of the receiver's partner should be just in front of or just behind the service line. The receiver's partner's first responsibility is to watch the serve and help her partner call deep serves as faults. Let your partner call the sidelines on the serve. The receiver's partner also needs to be ready to move in if the receiver hits a forcing return. If the

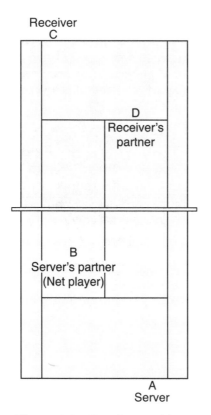

Figure 4.3 **Starting positions.**

return goes to the net player (the server's partner), the receiver's partner needs to be ready to retreat—fast.

The starting positions illustrated in figure 4.3 show one of the partners closer to the net than the other. This is known as one-up, one-back doubles and, at all levels of doubles play, points begin this way. But at more advanced levels, all four players do everything they can to take the net position from their opponents. The team at the net has a better chance of winning the point because they are more likely to be able to hit the ball downward. If you were in a street fight, wouldn't you rather be on top, hitting down than the reverse?

Another fascinating thing about the physics of tennis is that the closer you get to the net, the more angles you have to end the point (figure 4.4). To see these angles, move up to a foot (30.5 centimeters) from the net and see how easy it is to angle the ball sharply to the right or left out of reach of your opponents. Now take about six steps back, then six more, and notice how those same possibilities for angled shots disappear.

But let's get real. In most doubles play at the recreational level, one player is at the net and his partner is closer to the baseline. If that is not the optimal position, why do people do it? It really is a combination of factors:

- By the rules, the server and receiver must begin a point in the backcourt. It takes effort and skill to move closer to the net.
- Many players lack confidence in their net game. It takes time to develop the abilities to volley and hit an overhead smash in order to be confident at the net. Because most of us began tennis hitting ground strokes first, we often feel more secure playing in the backcourt.

So what if you want to play one-up, one-back doubles. We say, "Go for it!" If it is fun and you enjoy it, be our guest. You'll join millions of others who play the same way. The challenge comes when you come up against a team who is aggressive and takes the net from you. Now you have a problem. At the higher skill levels, almost all players move to the net as quickly as they can, so be prepared to take some lumps if you encounter these teams.

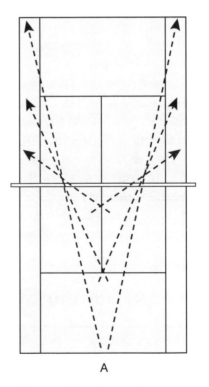

A

Figure 4.4 **Angles increase closer to the net.**

CHARGING THE NET

Many of us used to come to the net whenever possible. But alas, as age crept up, we found that charging the net repeatedly wasn't always wise. We become more susceptible to the lob as we get older, which makes charging the net a risky proposition. Our 25-inch (63.5-centimeter) vertical leap to smash an overhead turned into a 2-inch (5.1-centimeter) leap, at least some of the time. To compensate, we learned to come to midcourt and take more balls out of the air but not to close in quite so close to the net. In chapter 5, we will explain this in more detail.

A final word about one-up, one-back doubles. As you play more and improve your skills, it is fun to work on coming to the net more. But be patient. Playing the net takes time to learn, and smart players know how to pick the right time to move forward as a team to end the point. We'll give you ideas for how to do so in the next chapter.

Bisecting the Angle of Possible Returns

When we mention bisecting the angle of possible returns, some people get dizzy and others give us a blank look. But it is really just a simple application of the laws of physics.

When the ball is on the other side of the net, you and your partner should move into positions that bisect the possible shots from your opponent. Look at figure 4.5 to see the available angles of return and how both players together have cut that angle in half. That's what it means to bisect.

In the one-up, one-back formation, if the ball is placed deep into your opponent's deuce court, imagine the possible angles and cover them. If you are directly opposite the player who is playing the ball, you have two main responsibilities: to attack a weak return and try to end the point and to be alert for drives down the alley. Your partner, who is near the baseline, will cover a shot down the middle or a wide crosscourt angle.

Side-to-Side Movement as a Team

For your team to be in the optimal court position, you need to move together laterally so that you can always bisect the angle of possible shots (figure 4.6). Your cue is where the ball is on the other side of the net. If it lands in the deuce side of the court, both of you move to your left. If the next shot

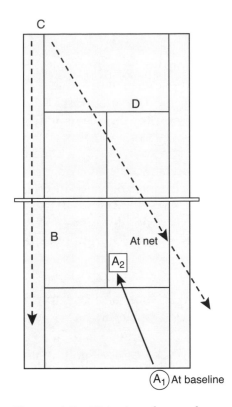

Figure 4.5 **Bisecting the angle as a team with one player up and one back (A1 shows player A in the back position) or with both players up at the net (A2 shows player A after he has moved to the net).**

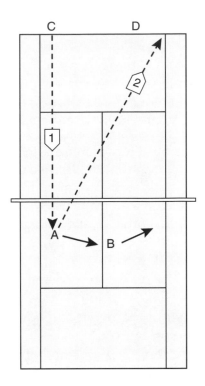

Figure 4.6 **At the net, players A and B move side to side to bisect the angle.**

lands in the ad side of the court, both of you move right. Shots that land in the middle call for both of you to crowd the middle.

While watching a doubles match, notice whether all four players move each time the ball is played. Accomplished players constantly adjust their court position by following the ball side to side. If you see one player moving to hit the ball and the other three players standing and watching, you are watching a lower level of play. And only one player gets to play at a time. That's not much fun or exercise.

Both you and your partner may end up at the net, by design or by accident. There's no need to panic. Move laterally to cover the possible shots just as you did in the one-up, one-back position. Generally, we like to see the person who is directly opposite the ball play a bit closer to the net while her partner shades about two steps back to guard against the lob. Note the positions of players A and B in figure 4.6.

Beginning the Point

Now that you've settled into the proper starting positions for play and understand the strategic principles of bisecting the angles of possible shots and moving side to side as a team, let's play a point. The two most critical shots are the serve and return of serve since these shots form the beginning of every point. Unless they are successful, the point ends.

Serving

All tennis points begin with a serve. Unlike in singles, in doubles the serving team has a huge advantage. The receiver has a smaller target for the return because if she hits it to the server's partner at the net, the serving team has a great chance to win the point.

The server's responsibilities are to get the ball in the service box, place the ball so it forces the receiver to use a weaker shot, and use spin to control the depth and pace of the serve. You don't have to hit monster serves, but you do have to get it in the box. The best strategy is to hit your first serve at about three-fourths speed to increase the odds of getting it in and make a real effort to place it to your opponent's weaker side, often the backhand.

STROKE DOCTOR

To place your serve, simply angle the racket face at contact in the direction you want the ball to go. The palm of your hand controls the racket face, so aim your palm at your target.

Most players at the 3.0 level and below have relatively weak second serves. This causes a lot of anxiety for the server's partner at the net who may face a scary return right at his navel. The solution to this dilemma is for the server to attempt to get a high percentage (about 70 percent) of first serves in. The receiving team will then be on the defensive, and the server's partner at the net will be grateful.

Flat serves that are hit with no spin usually miss the service box or have to be hit softly just to get them in. The more spin you apply to the ball, the harder you can swing and still get the ball to land in the service box. Here is where money for a lesson could be well spent along with a little practice time between playing matches.

STROKE DOCTOR

Work hard to develop spin on the serve. First, check your serving grip to be sure it is a continental grip. (See chapter 9 for information on grips.)

Next, imagine a clock face on the ball. Contacting the ball at about 2:00 on the imaginary clock face will impart a combination of topspin and sidespin to the ball.

Strategically, you have two choices for placing the serve: hit toward your opponent's weaker shot or play the percentages by aiming toward the inside third of the court. A serve to the inside of the court dictates a return that must travel back over the middle portion of the net. This kind of return is easier for the server's partner at the net to attack. In contrast, if you serve to the outside third of the court, your partner at the net has to move over to protect against the return down the alley, and you are left to cover the middle and the sharp angle crosscourt.

Vary your strategies during a match and see which is more effective, aiming for a stroke weakness or aiming for the inside third of the court. Your best choice will depend on how effectively you can place the serve and your opponents' skill.

Doubles is not much fun when the server double-faults. The serve is the one shot that is totally up to you, and your opponent cannot influence it. Take your time, have a plan, relax, and let it fly. If you're troubled by double faults, carefully reread chapter 3 on mental toughness; it could all be in your head.

Receiving Serve

The second shot of any point is the return of serve. The receiver's job is to get the ball in play, hit the ball crosscourt (usually), and force the serving team into a defensive shot.

At this level of play, the basic return is a crosscourt drive back to the server. Because the server will likely stay at the baseline, the receiver has two choices: hit a deep, aggressive shot that elicits a weak response, or aim the ball short into the service box and make the server run forward to play the ball. Both options are good depending on the strengths of the serving team. During a match try both, and stick with the one that seems most effective, or mix it up to keep your opponents guessing.

There are two major mistakes the receiver can make: plunking the ball into the net and hitting an easy shot to the net player, allowing the net player to hit a winner or tattoo the receiver's partner with the shot. Avoid these mistakes by aiming a few feet (half a meter or so) over the net and directing the ball crosscourt by angling your racket face in that direction.

If the speed, placement, or spin of your opponent's serve bothers you, you have a few options. Stand a little farther back to give yourself more time to swing, or shorten your swing. If neither of these options works, try lobbing over the head of the net player.

🎾 Practice Tip

Beginning a point is easy to practice. It takes only two people, perhaps you and your partner. One player serves and the other returns as if it were a doubles game. Concentrate on just these first two shots until you achieve the success you're looking for: a high percentage of well-placed first serves that land in and consistency in making returns of all types. To make this practice fun, serve one full game and keep track of how many times you get your first serve into the service box. The receiver should keep track of her number of successful returns. At the end of one game, switch roles just like in a match. To add difficulty, count only the serves that land in the inside third of the service box and returns that land crosscourt behind the service line.

Playing the Middle of the Point

Here is where the fun begins. If both the server and receiver are successful, the point becomes exciting. Now you can apply the principles of court positioning explained earlier. Once that becomes automatic, you can focus on choosing the right shot to hit. Study the next strategic principles carefully because they are the key to good doubles play and amazing points.

Deep to Deep, Short to Short

Assume both teams are in a one-up, one-back formation. In this formation, a good strategy is to apply the deep-to-deep, short-to-short principle (figure 4.7). This principle has three rules:

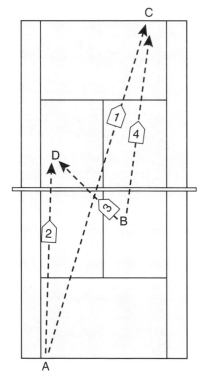

Figure 4.7 Deep-to-deep, short-to-short principle.

- Always play the ball deep to deep (shot 1).
- Hit short to short (shot 3) when you can hit the ball aggressively at your opponent's feet while in the short position.
- Aim short to deep (shot 4) if you are playing a ball defensively.

Of course, the unspoken and critical rule is to never hit deep to short (shot 2). That sets up the net player for a winning shot.

So why do so many players still try to hit a deep-to-short shot? Against a player who is fearful of playing a strong drive or has poor volley skills, hitting a deep-to-short shot may work. Some players may have experienced success with this shot. However, take our word for it, hitting at the net player may work at a beginning level, but by the time you reach the 3.0 level of skill, it is usually a terrible idea.

STROKE DOCTOR

If you are intimidated at the net when an opponent hits a hard drive at you, learn to defend yourself:

- During a point, expect every ball to come to you. Be especially alert and keep your racket in front.
- Keep your eye on the ball as your opponent hits it.
- Protect yourself from head to knees with your backhand volley. If you can get your racket face in front of you to deflect the oncoming shot, you will be safe and probably volley a winner.
- The most common mistake net players make on a shot hit right at them is to swing at the ball. It is better to just get the racket face in front of the oncoming ball.

Inside and Outside Balls

For the player at the net position, an inside ball is hit toward the center of the court, while an outside ball is played from the side closer to the sideline. In general, the strategic rule is to play inside balls back down the middle and play outside balls crosscourt (figure 4.8).

The reason for this is because a ball hit over the lowest part of the net (the middle) to the largest court angle has the highest chance of success and lowest risk. Of course, if you can close in to the net, the possible angles for shots become more attractive and less risky. If you are balanced and have an easy outside ball to play, you have our permission to play the ball straight down the line with an offensive volley.

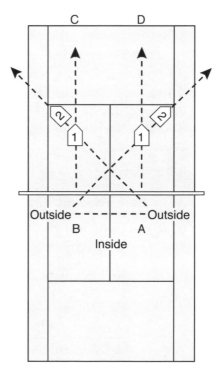

Figure 4.8 Inside and outside balls. Hit inside balls down the middle. Hit outside balls across the court.

Practice Tip

You will need four players to practice playing the middle of the point. Ignore the serve and return and begin by having the receiver feed the ball to the serving team. Play out points using the principles outlined in this chapter. First work on the deep-to-deep and short-to-short principle and evaluate your success. Then focus on where you direct inside and outside balls and again evaluate the result.

Aim Points

Think of the court as four quadrants. Those are the targets on which you want your shot to land. In doubles play, those four quadrants, plus a shot right down the middle, are the only places you ever have to hit the ball to win almost any point (figure 4.9). Notice that we haven't included the alleys as part of your targets. That's because the alleys provide your margin of error. If you miss your target by a few feet and it lands in the alley, fine. But if you aim for the alley (or even worse, a line) and miss by a few feet, your shot may be out.

Forget what the announcers say on television about professional players aiming shots for the line. They rarely do because they have learned the hard way to give themselves a decent margin of error. If they realize that fact, shouldn't we do the same?

If you follow the rule to aim points, it may take a shot or two longer to win the point. You'll be known as a smart, steady player, and you'll win a lot. The only downside is that you likely won't hit quite as many amazing winners that skip off the line. Oh well, that's the price of percentage tennis.

Shot Choice

The principles of good shot selection are common sense and are pretty clear:

- Hit your best, most effective shot whenever you can.
- Make your opponents hit their weakest shots as often as you can.
- Choose your shot, based on your court position (figure 4.10).

When in the backcourt (A1), lift the ball and apply spin for control. When in the midcourt (A2), hit the ball more on a straight line with less spin so that it penetrates through the court. When in the frontcourt (A3), contact the ball at the highest point you can and angle it downward.

If you are off balance, out of position, or deep behind the baseline, play a safe shot. A defensive lob is usually a good choice in these emergencies.

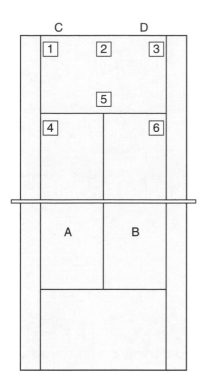

Figure 4.9   Aim points from the net position.

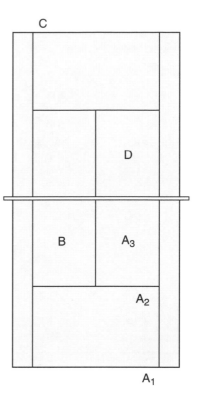

Figure 4.10   Shot selection based on court position. A1: flight up with topspin. A2: flight straight with little spin. A3: flight down with backspin.

If you are balanced and confident, play the ball more aggressively and apply spin for control. If you are in the backcourt and playing against net players, try to force them to hit a weak volley and then put away the next shot. Resist the temptation to try to win the point outright on your first shot. If your opponents have made two successful volleys and the ball is still in play, they will be looking to move closer to the net to make the next volley a winner. Lob the next shot to catch them moving in.

Ending the Point

Not many points last more than a couple of shots. Usually, one player makes a poor choice of shot or chooses the right shot but executes it badly. More points end on errors than on winning shots, but you still need to practice and know how to hit winners in doubles.

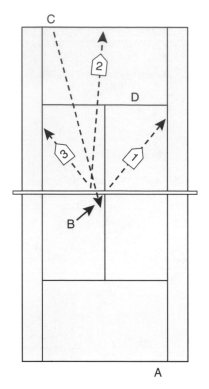

Figure 4.11 **Three choices for player B to end the point.**

The safest and easiest place to hit winners is from the net position. And the choices are simple (figure 4.11):

- Hit to an open part of the court (shot 1).
- Hit down the middle between your opponents (shot 2).
- Angle the ball sharply so that it crosses the sideline after the bounce (shot 3).

Choose the best shot depending on your court position (how close you are to the net), your opponents' court position, and the difficulty of the oncoming ball. Remember that earlier in this chapter, we advised you to play most inside balls (those hit to the center of the court) back down the middle and to aim most outside balls (those hit nearer the sideline) crosscourt. These rules will allow you to hit over the lowest part of the net and reduce errors on volleys. However, if you are able to get quite close to the net by anticipating an opponent's drive, more wide angles are open to either side of the court.

If you are able to close in close to the net, you have a great chance to win a point by angling the ball away across the sideline, especially if both opponents are back near the baseline. If one opponent is up and the other back, the shot with the highest percentage of winning the point is across the open diagonal between them. When you are farther back from the net or are facing a hard-hit ball with heavy topspin, the more sensible option is to play the ball deep down the middle of the court and wait for a better opportunity.

Practice Tip

Because most points are won at the net, that's where you should concentrate when practicing ending the point. Set targets on the court in the six recommended positions shown in figure 4.9 (page 53). Have your practice partner feed various types of balls to you at the net and aim for the on-court targets. Resist the tendency to overhit, but aim for a firm placement to the target. After 5 minutes, switch roles with your practice partner so that she gets to practice aiming for the targets.

It is also possible to hit winners from the backcourt, although the odds go down a bit. Your choices are shown in figure 4.12:

- Drive the ball down the middle between your opponents (shot 1). Both or neither of them may try to play the ball, both good results for you. This shot should be your first choice.

- Lob over the head of players who have come to the net (shot 2). Remember, as players age, it becomes more difficult for them to retreat than to go forward. The lob is generally your second choice.

- The third and most risky shot is to try to pass an opponent with a shot down the alley (shot 3).

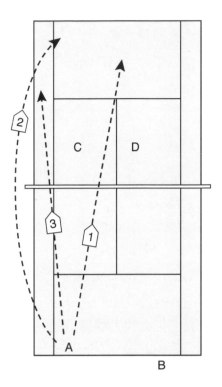

Figure 4.12 Three choices for player A to end the point.

Many players at this level insist on trying to pass the net player by aiming the shot down the alley. The odds of success are poor unless the net player has been crossing or cheating toward the middle to try to pick off balls. The other possible reason for hitting down the alley is if the net player lacks skill or confidence in his volley. We recommend trying this shot a few times in a match to keep the net player honest, especially if he is looking to poach. If he is no threat to shots down the middle, then you can simply ignore him and aim for the larger target in the middle of the court between the two opponents.

The chart "High-Percentage Shots in Doubles" lists the shots for doubles with the highest percentage of success based on the strategy of the game. These are the fundamentally sound shots that every doubles player should learn and practice first. Of course, you might change these strategies based on your strengths and weaknesses and your opponents' strengths and weaknesses. Those tactical adjustments are what make this game fun.

A final word about team strategy. Doubles teams should agree on three key rules if they expect to cover the court cooperatively:

One up, one back: In this case, the player closer to the net always has priority on every shot, even a shot on the other side of the court if she can

HIGH-PERCENTAGE SHOTS IN DOUBLES

GAME SITUATION	BEST SHOT

Serving
  Server
  Net player
	Hit inside third of service box or to opponent's weakness.
	Hit crosscourt diagonal or at receiver's partner's feet.

Receiving
  Receiver
  Receiver's partner
	Hit crosscourt.
	Hit down the middle.

Returning inside balls	Hit down the middle.
Returning outside balls	Hit crosscourt at an angle.
At baseline with opponents in one-up, one-back formation	Hit crosscourt and away from net player.
At baseline with both opponents at the net	Hit low down the middle.
At net with opponents in one-up, one-back formation	Hit at net player's feet or deep.
At net with both opponents deep	Hit down the middle or angle across sideline.
Lobbing	Hit crosscourt diagonal or over net player's backhand side.
Hitting overhead smash	Hit crosscourt diagonal.

reach it, because the net player has a better chance of hitting a winner than the player farther back. One exception might be a ball that is below the net. That ball may be better left to the partner behind the net player.

Both players at the net: When the ball is in your opponents' court, the net player on the opponents' side of the court has two jobs: pick off a weak shot above the net and defend against a shot down the alley. His partner, who is diagonally opposite the ball, must first cover the middle shot (figure 4.13) by moving toward that side of the court. A smart opponent who is pulled wide of the sideline may be able to hit a sharp crosscourt angle, but that is the lower-percentage shot. Cover the middle first.

Lobs: Both players should try to cover their own lobs by anticipating them, backing up quickly, and hitting an overhead or lobbing back to the opponents. However, sometimes a net player has closed into the net and cannot retreat quickly enough. In this case, she should yell "yours" and hope her partner can cross diagonally to intercept the lob. Normally, after a lob goes over your head, you will want to retreat to the baseline with your partner.

Basic Team Talk

A successful doubles team finds that communicating effectively helps them work together smoothly, instills confidence, and makes the match more fun. Here are the key points of good doubles communication:

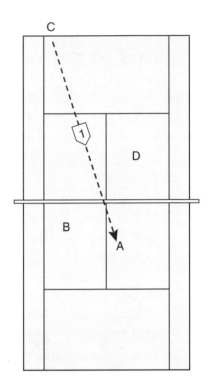

Figure 4.13 **The player who is diagonally opposite the ball covers the shot down the middle.**

- Before every point, make sure both of you know the correct score, whether you are the serving team or the receiving team.

- During the point, help your partner let balls go by calling "out" when you are sure the ball will land outside the court.

- During the point, call "yours" if you want your partner to take an overhead smash or cover a lob that is over your head.

- During the point, if both of you are at the baseline defending, call "mine" or "yours" on any shot down the middle.

- During the point, if you play a defensive lob, warn your partner to move back to defend.

- After the point, applaud good shots and high-five great shots. If your partner misses a shot, encourage him to hang in there and get the next one. Simply saying "bad luck" is often a terrific reassurance.

- When you change ends of the court, briefly suggest changes in tactics you think might work and agree as a team what your plan of attack will be.

- At the end of a match, thank your partner for playing and compliment her on her effort and any outstanding plays she made no matter which team won.

WORDS TO THE WISE

- Begin each point in the recommended starting position and know where you plan to move as the point develops.
- As a doubles team, learn where to move to bisect the angles of possible shots from your opponents.
- Move laterally as a team to bisect the angles.
- When the point begins, adopt the strategy of consistency and placement to give your opponents a chance to make an error.
- In the middle of the point, use the deep-to-deep, short-to-short principle. Remember what to do with inside and outside balls and how to choose the best shot to fit the situation.
- To end the point from the net, aim for the open court or at the feet of your opponent. To end the point from the baseline, drive down the middle between your opponents or lob over their heads.
- Use basic communication skills throughout the match to keep yourself and your partner working together toward common goals and tactics.

CHAPTER

5

Advanced Doubles Strategy and Tactics

This chapter primarily benefits players at the National Tennis Rating Program (NTRP) level of 3.5 and above. Most players who have played tennis continuously at some time in their lives will have reached this level. Even players who may have been rated as high as 5.0 at one time find that as they move into their late 50s and early 60s they have moved down a level or two in order to compete with younger players. Happily, the United States Tennis Association also has levels with age categories. You might enjoy playing at the 4.5 level for people 50 years of age and older. That eliminates players who are younger, stronger, and more fleet of foot.

At the 3.5 level of play and above, most players have eliminated glaring stroke weaknesses in their game, although they may still have a limited repertoire of shots to choose from. Most strokes are somewhat grooved and can be hit consistently, and players at these levels can control the height, direction, depth, and speed of their shots. However, there is still significant room for improvement in accuracy, variety, power, and disguise of at least some of their shots.

Compared to players who are rated 3.0 and below, higher-skilled players often have one or two strengths, which may be a particular stroke, such as the forehand; general net play; or court movement and coverage. To move up a level, players at 3.5 and 4.0 often need to add one or more shots to give them a more complete game.

Because of their higher level of skill, implementing more advanced strategies and tactics comes naturally to players at this level. Both offensive and defensive positions and tactics can be tailored to specific opponents and can even be adjusted during a match. Years of play against many types of players have also prepared players at this level to adjust to playing a left-handed opponent, a big server, aggressive net players, or those who push every ball back into play.

In this chapter, we cover the 80–20 principle of shot selection, offensive and defensive strategy, shot variety, team communication, strategic adjustments for players 50 years of age and older, and doubles styles of play.

80–20 Principle

The 80–20 principle is a helpful doubles strategy that can help you choose the best shot in any situation. (The principle can also be used during singles.) Simply stated, the 80–20 principle means that 80 percent of the time, you will choose the best-percentage shot (as shown on the chart "High Percentage Shots in Doubles" on page 56), the shot that is likely to force an error from your opponents or cause you to win the point outright. The other 20 percent of the time, you will choose a shot that you'd like to try even though the odds of success may be lower. The thrill of pulling off a lower-percentage shot will give you something to brag about after the match and keep you coming back for more. Even if you miss the shot, your opponents will know that you may try it again, and they have to factor that into their defensive game.

If you are playing a serious, competitive match, your partner will thank you for restricting the number of lower-percentage shots. On points that could win or lose a game or a match, they are a particularly bad idea. We advise you to save those lower-percentage shots for situations in which your team is clearly dominating a match or you believe the risk is necessary to keep your opponents off balance by hitting an unexpected shot. A good example is a drop shot or drop volley that lands softly over the net. If you catch your opponents by surprise, it can be a winner, but if they anticipate it, your partner may end up in a helpless position.

You also should keep a mental tally of your shots during a match and have a sense of when it might be wise to change the pattern. For example, if you have been returning serve crosscourt effectively and consistently, your opponents will begin to anticipate that shot, and the net player may begin poaching your return. This is the time to cross them up by lobbing the return of serve over the net player, eliminating his poach and catching them both by surprise.

We suggest you also try lower-percentage shots during practice matches so that you can improve your technique and confidence in the shot. Then when you attempt it in a meaningful match, your chances of success will be significantly increased.

Doubles Offensive Strategy

The largest difference in play at the 3.5 NTRP level and above is in the strategic play at the net position. Most players at this level play more aggressively at the net, serve and volley at least occasionally, know how to poach, and use alternative team formations at the net.

Serve and Volley

In doubles, the serving team begins the point with the advantage of the server's partner already positioned at the net. If the server can join his partner at the net after the serve, the team can take the offensive net position as a team just like the pros do.

However, it is not an advantage to the serving team to rush the net after a weak serve. Try varying your serving position at the baseline to create different angles and give the receiver a different look. Like a savvy veteran baseball pitcher, mix up the spin, speed, and placement of the serve to keep the receiver off balance and guessing.

STROKE DOCTOR

When serving, be careful not to fall into a predictable pattern by hitting the first serve hard and the second serve softly. Vary your pattern by serving softly to the opponent's weaker shot on the first serve. Similarly, some players always hit the first serve wide to the outside third of the court and the second to the inside third. Reverse that pattern occasionally to keep the receiver off balance. Another strategy that works well against many players is to serve right at the receiver's body, forcing her to move out of the way to play the return.

You may want to serve and volley only on first serves or only on certain points. You might find success by serving and volleying against one opponent but not the other. Some players prefer doing it only when they are ahead in the game or when they have the advantage point. This tactic may earn you the point, and even if it fails, you are still in the game and you've added an element of surprise for the receiver to consider on

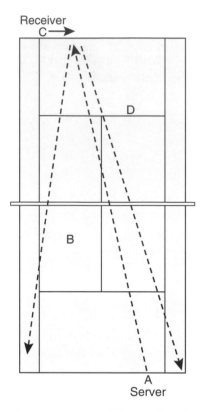

Receiver
C →
D
B
A
Server

Figure 5.1 **Possible angle of returns of a serve to the inside third of the service box.**

subsequent points. The receiver who expects you to come to the net may hit a short return that is just perfect for you to play as an approach shot and then take the net. If the receiver expects you to stay at the baseline, chances are the return will be higher and allow you to hit a more comfortable volley.

In doubles, the best strategic aim point for the serve is the inside third of the service box nearest the centerline. Figure 5.1 shows the possible return angles for the receiver on a serve to the inside third of the service box. The return must come back over the middle third of the net, making it easier for the server and the server's partner to anticipate and attack a weak return.

Another effective serving strategy is to serve toward the receiver's body. Some receivers have a difficult time moving out of the line of flight to play the ball comfortably, and they dread a serve coming right at the body.

What about the wide serve to the outside third of the service box? A wide serve can be effective if the receiver is weaker on that side or is expecting a serve inside. The key is to disguise the serve by using the same toss position for every serve. Also, it's a great idea to warn your partner if you plan to serve wide to the outside of the court so that she can move to the outside to protect against a return down the alley.

Net Play

The net player of the serving team can have a dramatic impact on play. If your partner is serving, you have priority on any ball. Because you are closer to the net, more angles are available to you, and you have a better chance of winning the point outright. Offensively, you should be ready to make two key moves.

Poach: Cut across the net to intercept a crosscourt return. The best poaches are planned in advance. Signal your partner that you plan to go (figure 5.2). Once the signal is given, it is your responsibility to move just as the receiver is ready to play the return and keep going. No retreat is allowed because your partner should be covering the other half of the court.

Drift: This is a safer play than a poach. Wait to see the direction of the ball and the type of shot. If the return appears to be relatively weak, explode toward the net to pick it off. If the return is below the net or angled wide, let it go for your partner to play. A drift is a reaction to a poor return and therefore you cannot signal a drift ahead of time to your partner.

When you poach or drift, move on a 45-degree angle toward the net (figure 5.3). This reduces your distance to the ball so you can contact the ball earlier in flight, giving your opponents less time to react and providing more target angles from which to choose.

Figure 5.2 **Net player giving a poaching signal.**

The net player has two other responsibilities. The net player must be ready for a shot down the line, especially if the serve is weak or he has moved across to poach on previous points. Also the net player must anticipate a lob return and retreat quickly to play an overhead smash if possible. If the lob is over your head, try to retrieve it or call for your partner to cover it for you.

The offensive net player has plenty to do. Develop a plan with your serving partner. If you simply stand in a stationary position at the net while your partner plays the second shot, you may find yourself looking for a new partner.

Alternative Net Positions

At times, it is strategically wise to play the Australian formation at the net. Figure 5.4 shows the net player (player B) near the centerline but on the same side as the server, which is the opposite side of the court from the usual position. This strategy takes away the crosscourt return of service from the receiving team. It also forces them to hit down the line over the higher part of the net. The distance to the baseline is shorter than on a crosscourt return. It may just psych them out.

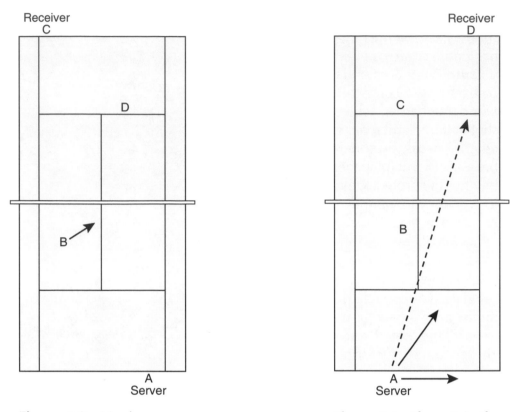

Figure 5.3 Moving on a 45-degree angle to poach or drift.

Figure 5.4 Player B in the Australian net position.

Another strategy is to play in the I formation. In the I formation, the net player is directly in front of the server, but crouched at the net (figure 5.5). As the serve lands in the service box, the net player moves right or left, confusing the receiver. It is a good idea to use both the Australian and I formations to increase the choices for the receiver, particularly if your team is having difficulty winning service games.

Note: If you can crouch low enough in the I formation to avoid being hit by the serve, you are still on the young side of 50. If your knees still bend comfortably, go for it. For most of us, however, this position is a memory. We'll have to stick with a conventional position or use the Australian for variety.

Team Coverage of the Net

When you and your partner are both in net positions, assume a staggered position. That is, one of you should be closer to the net and the other a few steps back. Which player is closer to the net depends on where the ball is on the other side of the net.

As described in chapter 4, you need to bisect the angle of possible shots by your opponent. Here is how it works when you are both at the net. If the ball is deep on the other side of the net, the ball-side player (player A) takes a position closer to the net than her partner (figure 5.6). Player A's responsibility is to pick off a weak return and protect her alley. Her partner's job (player B) is to play any shot down the middle.

If the ball is short on the other side, the ball-side player (player A) should retreat a few steps to protect the alley and be ready to play a ball down the middle (figure 5.7). Her partner (player B) should close in to cut off the sharp angle of possible shots because the ball landed short on the other side. Because she has closed in, a ball that pops up weakly in the middle also gives her a chance to hit a forcing volley.

How do you cover a lob if you and your partner are both at the net? Make every effort to hit an overhead smash first. If the ball is over your head, see if you can retrieve it yourself or call "yours" and hope

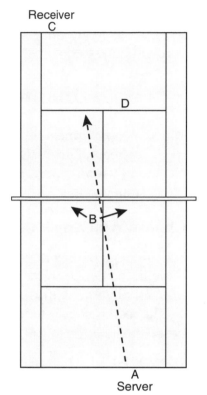

Figure 5.5 I formation at the net.

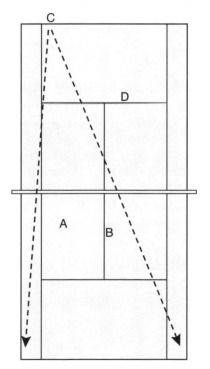

Figure 5.6 Defending against a deep shot.

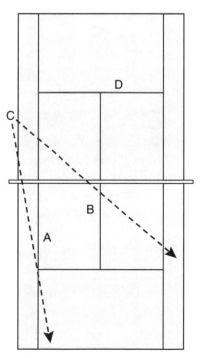

Figure 5.7 Defending against a short-angle shot.

your partner can cover it for you. As you play together as a team, you'll soon learn favorite shots and weaknesses and you can anticipate which of you will have to do most of the scrambling to cover lobs.

Doubles Defensive Strategy

You and your partner will have to play defense, especially when you are the receiving team. Our personalities are exposed on the tennis court: Some of us naturally tend toward offense and others toward defense. The following offers strategic advice for when you are on defense.

Choose Which Side of the Court to Play

You and your partner need to make a smart decision about who will receive serve in the deuce and ad courts. You've probably heard arguments about the best alignment, most of which are simply generalizations.

The best strategy is to have each partner play on the side he or she plays best. Consider the following factors:

- Choose the side based on how well both players can return serve at their level of play.

- Ignore advice about forehand and backhand strengths; that only works if the server accommodates you by serving to your strength. Many players with strong forehands prefer to play the deuce court, but if the server can consistently hit to the inside of the service box (as he or she should), you'll never see a forehand return.

- Lefty and righty combinations should follow the same principle—play the side you play best. Forehands in the middle and forehands on the outside are not necessarily convincing reasons. What if one player has a better backhand than forehand?

- Some coaches will advise you to play the stronger player on the ad side because all pressure points will occur there. Actually, you can also make an argument for putting the stronger player on the deuce side because if she gives you a lead in every game by winning the first and third points, the pressure shifts to the serving team, not your partner.

- After the return of serve, the player whose strong shots are forehand drives, forehand volleys, and overhead smashes should play on the ad side. On the ad side, she would naturally get to use those shots more.

- Over time, players tend to adjust to the side they play best on returns and rallies and when at the net. Every player should make an effort to become equally confident playing on both sides to open up more possibilities, regardless of the partner.

Receiver's Partner

As we mentioned in chapter 4, the receiver's partner has to help call the serve in or out and then immediately be prepared to move either forward or back depending on the quality of the return. A mistake often made by the receiver's partner is to look back at the receiver to watch the return. A better plan is, after determining that the serve is good, to shift your eyes immediately to the net player on the other side to see if he will play the ball. If he has an easy shot, it is probably coming in your direction. Quickly move back a few steps and hold your ground so that you can protect yourself and get your racket on the ball.

If the net player shows no sign of movement, look at the server. If he is moving in and playing a high volley, follow the same advice. Retreat, stop to regain your balance, and be ready for anything.

STROKE DOCTOR

Keep the eyes forward always! The receiver's partner should watch the opponents so that she can be in the best position to return their volleys. In fact, you should always watch your opponents throughout a point so that you can anticipate their next shot. Never look back to watch your partner play the shot. By the time you shift your eyes forward, it is too late to react.

Receiver's Partner Poach

If a serve (particularly a second serve) is relatively weak, the receiver should be able to drive the return and put the server on the defensive. That opens up the possibility for the receiver's partner to poach the next shot by moving across to intercept it. If the server stays at the baseline after his serve, begin your poach just as he begins his forward swing for the shot. If the server follows his serve to the net but has to play the ball from below the net, as soon as you see him bending to reach the ball, move in and across to intercept his shot.

Remember that the player closer to the net has priority on every ball. If you anticipate a weak return, make sure you move diagonally forward to poach (figure 5.8). Some players make the mistake of moving laterally across the court and usually miss the shot as a result. Aim your poach down the middle or at the feet of the net player on the other side.

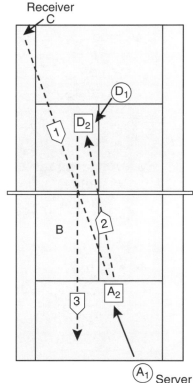

Figure 5.8 **Receiver's partner (player D) poaching.**

Typically, partners don't signal a receiver's partner poach because the poach depends on the quality of the return and therefore is more like the drift described earlier. But it is a good idea for the receiver to alert her partner if she is not going to drive crosscourt but instead plans to hit down the line or lob the return. In those cases, there is no possibility of a poach and the receiver's partner should be ready to defend against the net player's volley or smash.

Two-Back Formation

If the serving team is abusing the receiver's partner by poaching, drifting, or hitting overhead smashes, the receiver's partner should move back toward the baseline to begin the point. Take a position just inside the baseline so that you can move quickly up or back (figure 5.9). Although this takes away the potential net position or a receiver poach, the receiver's partner will gain time and remove a prime target for the opposing net players. If the serving team continues to hit the same volleys, the receiver's partner is now in position to play them with a drive or a lob.

This formation is a smart choice if you or your partner have difficulty returning serve. The receiver only has to make sure the ball gets over the net and then both of you can defend from the baseline.

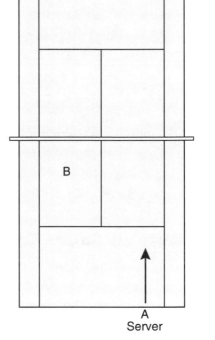

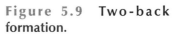

Figure 5.9 Two-back formation.

Defense Against a Net Player

There are a number of ploys to neutralize an aggressive net player on the other team. Try these strategies against a player who poaches often:

- Hit down the line occasionally to keep him honest.
- Lob down the line, over his head, preferably to the backhand side.
- Lob deep to the middle of the backcourt.
- Drive the ball with pace right at him.
- Move in to return serve, and chip the ball low over the net.

The strategy you choose depends on your strengths. If you are a clever lobber, use lobs against aggressive net players. If you have a powerful, driving ground stroke, punish the net player by putting her on the defense.

Shot Variety

In tennis, most points are won on errors, not winners. If you keep your opponents guessing by varying the pace, spin, direction, and height of your shots, they will make mistakes. Lob into the sun or wind and let them figure out how to play the ball. Give them pace and follow it with a lob or short chip. Aim for the middle on most shots, but go down the line enough that they cannot anticipate every shot.

Vary your starting position when you are the serving team and when you are receiving. Once the point begins, don't just react to your opponents' shots. Move without the ball to bisect angles, and move across the court at the net to intercept a weak shot that can be hit aggressively.

Some alternative positions for serving include moving closer to the center or wide to create different serving angles (figure 5.10). Of course, the receiver should adjust her position so that the angle of possible serves can be bisected. The partners of the server and the receiver may vary their positions by moving forward to a more aggressive net position if they anticipate a weak shot or by moving backward to defend against offensive shots or lobs.

Check yourself during a match to see whether you are varying your shots enough to keep your opponents off balance. We've seen doubles teams play an entire match without ever hitting down the line or lobbing the return of serve. Even if the shot is not successful, the variation prevents your opponents from anticipating your next shot.

If you are losing a match, discuss possible tactical changes with your partner. You may need to be more aggressive, use more angles to win points, play more balls to the weaker player, lob to back your opponents away from the net, or vary your serving placement patterns. If the score is close, you may be better off sticking with your plan but focusing on improving your execution of the strategy. However, if you are badly behind in the score, more drastic tactical adjustments probably make sense.

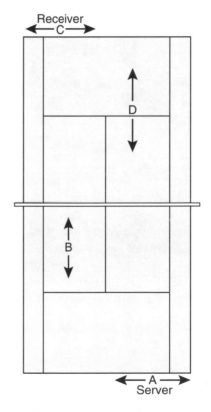

Figure 5.10 Alternative serving and receiving positions.

Team Talk

In chapter 4, we suggested ways to enhance communication with a partner, advice that is applicable for players at every level of play. If you skimmed that chapter, refer back to it to review the principles of good teamwork and communication.

At the 3.5 level and above, players have a higher degree of skill and a more varied game, and usually they can employ different strategies and tactics within a match to confuse opponents. As that happens, you and your partner need to work closely as a team to neutralize your opponents' strengths and probe for their weaknesses.

Before the match, discuss your team goals for the match and agree on a general tactical approach such as "We need to be aggressive and take the net away from them." If your opponents are notorious slow starters, you may want to let them serve first and put pressure on them early in the match. Whatever plan you come up with is better than no plan at all. Imagine a football or basketball team going out with no game plan in mind.

Good doubles teams talk before, during, and after a match.

During the match, you may need to make tactical changes. But often it is an attitude adjustment or energy change that one or both of you need. You need to understand how to raise your arousal level as a team or relax together when you feel pressure. To raise your arousal level, move more quickly, bounce on your toes, move more aggressively to intercept balls, and hustle to retrieve every shot. If you need to lower your arousal level, try to coax a smile, use humor, reassure each other, and avoid placing blame for past failures. Focus on the present, review your tactical plan, and concentrate on executing it.

Some players don't call the score because they think it's not macho and others because they forget or don't know the score. These are all poor excuses. The server should call the score and the other three players confirm or challenge her throughout the match. If there are score tenders on the court, use them and put up the correct score after every odd game as you change ends of the court.

After the match, spend time with your partner to review the things you did well as a team and identify areas of improvement. Be gentle but honest with yourself and each other. Resolve to spend time practicing together to smooth out rough spots before the next match. Express your appreciation for your partner's effort. Once you've reviewed the match, let it go. Look ahead to the next time you can play as a team.

If a match was particularly close and hard fought, some people need time to relax, reflect, and get their emotions under control. If that describes you or your partner, shake hands, have some refreshments, and postpone the talk until a better time. If your partner is also your spouse, aim for positive comments and make the suggestions carefully, or maybe not at all.

Adjusting Doubles Strategy After Age 50

It is inevitable that you'll have to make changes to your tennis game as you age. The rate of change is different for each person, but some general principles may help guide you. Here are our observations of how players change their game over the years. Happily, these changes don't mean your skills have regressed. You've just added new ones and modified your strategic options.

Variety, placement, and accuracy begin to replace power and speed as you age. Begin now to work on your tennis technique so that you will have a full range of options. Take your cue from professional athletes who learn to maximize their ability to compete as they age by emphasizing different skills. This may be the time to enlist the aid of a teaching professional to add a new shot to your arsenal. With her help, you will learn the new shot more quickly and the shot will be more technically sound. In the following chapter on stroke technique for doubles play, you'll learn about doubles shots that you might like to add.

Players over 50 tend to hit fewer outright winners because the speed of their shots declines, and they compensate for the lack of winners by making fewer unforced mistakes. Expect every point to last longer, especially if you are playing on a soft, slow court surface. You'll find that even well-struck shots down the center of the court are returned, so you must develop the ability to angle shots across the sideline to end the point. This is a more advanced skill and requires smart positioning, good touch, and clean racket work.

Serving and Receiving

Hard, flat serves are probably just a memory now or soon will be. The stress on your arm and shoulder are simply too much for repetitive serves at a high rate of speed. It's much better to improve your serve by improving placement and by adding depth, different spins, and more variety. You should be able to place your serve in each of the three areas of the service box—the inside, center, and outside third—on both the deuce and ad sides of the court. We'd venture to guess that most of you haven't mastered those six serves.

Perhaps the most dramatic improvement you can make is to improve your second serve. If you can spin it deep into the court, even under pressure, then you can take more risks on the first serve by aiming closer to the lines. If you still hit your second serve slower than your first one, make it a priority to learn how to apply spin to the ball to allow you to hit out on the second serve and still depend on it to land in the court.

As a receiver, your primary objective is to get the ball back in play. Once you can do that consistently, about 8 times out of 10, you need to change your focus to trying to force an error or weak shot from your opponent. Check yourself to see if you can consistently return crosscourt out of the reach of the net player, down the line to keep her honest, and with a lob over the net player's backhand side.

A final note for both serving and receiving. Have a coach or playing buddies check your ability to disguise your shots. You'd like to be able to play several different types of shots with the same preparation so that your opponent cannot anticipate which shot is coming. You may be tipping off your opponent with your posture, shoulder turn, lack of shoulder turn, or your body weight moving forward or back as you hit the ball. Practice hitting all your shots with identical preparation, body balance, and shoulder turn until they look much the same.

Moving Without the Ball

Have you ever watched a skilled senior tennis player and marveled at how little he seems to run yet he seems to get to every shot. Here's his secret: Smart players move while the ball is on the other side of the net to get into the best possible position to play the next shot. They decide where to move depending on the location of the ball on the other side and whether it lands short, deep, in the middle, or on one side. Together with their partner, they then bisect the angle of possible returns.

A smart player has a brain like a computer that stores information gathered from previous points and matches. You can almost predict your opponent's next shot by calling up the memory of what he did in previous similar situations, what the best-percentage shot might be, and his arsenal of tennis shots. Mix all that information together and move to where you expect the next shot to land.

The difference between experienced players and those at lower skill levels is not how much they move, but when they move. Younger players sometimes compensate for being out of position by hustling after shots after they land on their side of the net. But veterans know that the key time to move is while the ball is on the other side of the net. That's when you should be moving.

Shrinking the Court

As your mobility decreases and you are able to cover less court space, it's essential that you shrink the court. You can accomplish this by moving forward to cut off angles and playing more balls from the midcourt. We'll explain how.

When you are at the baseline, position yourself a few feet inside the baseline. From there, you can easily move forward or back a few steps to play any shot. If you insist on staying behind the baseline, you'll be susceptible to drop shots, drop volleys, and short angles.

When you are at the net, if your opponent proves that she will lob with some frequency, back off the net to a position a few steps behind the normal starting position in the center of the service box. That small position adjustment makes it easier to reach lobs with your overhead smash or retrieve a lob over your head. If your opponents drive the ball to you, there is still time to move in two steps to play the volley if you anticipate the shot.

The middle of the court used to be referred to as no man's land. Then it became no person's land. After age 50, it must become a key position for you and your partner. If coaches used to tell you to move through midcourt quickly on your way to the net or back to the baseline, you now have to adjust your thinking and realize that midcourt is not such a bad place to be (figure 5.11). It's just a matter of learning how to play balls from the midcourt.

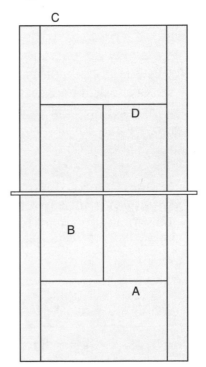

Figure 5.11 **Players A and D playing in midcourt.**

You'll easily be able to play deep drives and lobs while standing in midcourt. Drop shots, drop volleys, and sharply angled shots are reachable with a few steps. The only shots that are problematic are those that land at your feet. That requires that you work especially hard to take balls on the short hop or half-volley. This skill is essential for older players and relatively easy to learn with expert coaching and a little practice.

The other key shot from the midcourt is an approach volley. You hit it much like a normal approach shot, except that you contact it in the air with a medium-size swing (about a three on a scale of zero to five) and some backspin for control. Play the ball while moving forward, and follow it to the net.

Keeping Your Eyes on the Ball

Another suggestion for players over 50 is to have your eyes checked regularly and wear corrective lenses if you have a vision deficiency. Seeing the ball well is crucial to playing well, and you'll make better line calls, too.

After age 40, there are clear changes in functional vision. The amount of light that reaches the retina is reduced, producing difficulty in focusing on near objects. Tracking a tennis ball hit at high speed becomes more challenging, and if you wear bifocals, the challenge is heightened.

Regular eye examinations will reveal deterioration in your visual capacities or the presence of disease. The most common age-related eye diseases are macular degeneration, cataracts, glaucoma, and diabetic retinopathy. A trusted ophthalmologist can help you prevent or treat these diseases.

If your vision becomes problematic and you have ruled out disease or adopted a treatment plan, what else can you do? Our best advice is to choose times to play when natural light is at its best. Playing at dusk or under lights at outdoor and at many indoor clubs will strain your visual ability.

If these strategies aren't an option, adjust your play. Let more lobs bounce before you try to hit overheads. Play back from the net a bit to give yourself more time to react to the oncoming ball. And keep in mind that your opponents are battling the same issues, so it is up to you to make the best adjustment you can.

Doubles Styles of Play

Just as players prefer different styles in singles, players prefer to play different doubles styles. We classify them as offensive, defensive, and all-around.

Typically, the offensive doubles player loves to play the net, poaches aggressively, hits the ball with pace, and loves to hit winning shots. A defensive player is more content to hit every shot back to the opponent, makes few mistakes, and loves to frustrate an offensive player with lobs, spins, clever placements, and balls with little pace. All-around doubles players are experienced, well-rounded shotmakers who can shift easily from offense to defense and back. They can play with most partners and change their style of play to adjust to specific opponents.

Many doubles teams are formed by two players who have different styles of play. An offensive partner will value her partner's steady play that allows her to be aggressive. The reliable defensive player needs the offensive player to end points that might otherwise last forever.

We've seen good doubles teams of two offensive players, two defensive players, or one of each. It is not the style of play that determines the success of the team, but the players' ability to blend their personalities and skills and use teamwork to accomplish their strategic plan. The important thing is to play the style of play that suits your personality and shot-making ability.

WORDS TO THE WISE

- Play the best-percentage shot 80 percent of the time and use the other 20 percent to aim for more risky shots so you have something to brag about after the match (if you make them!).

- Playing at the net in doubles is the key to an offensive game plan. Work on your positioning, formations, team movement, and net skills to gain the offensive.

- Defensive skills can foil the opposing team's plan of attack and keep you in the match. Sometimes a good offense is simply a great defense.

- As the years roll by, it is essential to make strategic adjustments.

- Blend your style of doubles play with your partner's style to develop a unique style that emphasizes both players' strengths and covers up weaknesses.

Technique Skills for Doubles

As a skill sport, tennis demands that you acquire the racket skills to achieve your strategic objectives. As we age, technique rises in importance so we can produce efficient strokes that achieve our objectives with minimum effort and strength. Just a few years ago, we might have relied on our natural athleticism to play tennis, but as time diminishes some of our explosiveness, we need to compensate with more precise, efficient strokes.

All the strategy you learned in the previous two chapters will be useless unless you can execute your plan. This chapter is devoted to helping you improve your doubles tennis skills and perhaps add a few new shots.

This chapter covers the following topics and more:

- Understanding tennis skill technique
- Controlling the flight of the ball
- Recognizing the difference between errors of choice and errors of execution and learning to correct them
- Learning the best all-purpose doubles shot and specialty shots
- Practicing doubles skills

Understanding Tennis Skill Technique

Although you may be able to make adjustments to your shots through self-analysis and practice, we believe you can speed the learning process with professional help from an experienced, certified tennis coach. The best way for beginners to learn doubles skills is to join a group of people who are just learning to play doubles. Usually, a teaching professional will demonstrate and explain the four starting positions to begin the point and work with the group to learn to execute those shots. Another approach is to work on the middle of points first to eliminate the serve and return until you've had a chance to practice those skills. If you are an experienced player, working with a tennis professional is still the quickest route to improving your skills. A good coach or professional can quickly pick out stroke flaws, suggest a remedy, and provide feedback to you as you change or remake a stroke.

Even novice players can begin playing a modified game of doubles during their first experience on the court. If your instructor presents each of the skills in the context of playing a point, the skills make more sense because the objective is clear. As you learned earlier in this book, this approach is called game-based teaching.

The best thing about learning doubles in a group situation is that you have playing partners immediately available during the lesson. And you've made new acquaintances at your skill level with whom you can play outside your instructional time.

If you have played tennis for some time and are reasonably skilled at doubles, you can still benefit from joining an instructional clinic or an adult team practice. This chapter helps you evaluate your current tennis technique and perhaps expose areas that you will want to improve. We present suggestions that will help make your shots more consistent and effective. We also suggest new skills that you may want to add to your repertoire.

Basic Tennis Techniques

Figure 6.1 summarizes the key points of tennis technique for any shot. Use this chart to evaluate your current technique and plan improvements through instruction or practice. We've divided overall technique into three headings: preparation for the shot, racket technique, and body control. Let's take a look at each category.

Prepare for the Shot

This part of the shot will challenge your senses, mind, and experience. If you absorbed some of the information on tennis strategy, you already

Preparation for the Shot

- Anticipate the shot and move into the best position.
- Judge the ball flight, speed and spin.
- Set up to play the ball in balanced position.

Racket Technique

- Prepare the racket with a unit turn.
- Determine the size of the backswing needed.
- Time the impact of the ball with the racket.
- Finish the shot and recover for the next shot.

Body Control

- Use a split-step to change direction.
- Keep the body balanced throughout the execution of the shot.
- Keep muscle tension at an appropriate level.
- Keep your head still during the shot.

Figure 6.1   Summary of overall tennis technique.

know a few of the secrets of anticipation because you understand what your opponent is likely to do in every situation. Your first responsibility is to move without the ball before your opponent even strikes the shot. Remember to move to bisect the angles of possible shots from your opponent who is playing the ball.

Now your senses come into play. Look and listen as your opponent plays the ball. Notice the height of the shot over the net, the speed it was hit, and the spin on the ball. Each of those cues will help you determine your final steps to get into the best position to hit your shot.

STROKE DOCTOR

Focus on your opponent as she swings and judge these three factors:

- A short or slow backswing means the ball will come to you more slowly than a ball hit with a full swing or fast swing.
- The height of the shot will affect the depth when it lands on your side of the net. Be ready to move back for higher shots and forward for those that just skim the net.

- The path of the racket swing determines the spin on the ball. A low-to-high swing will produce topspin; a high-to-low swing produces backspin.

Use these three cues together to gauge the oncoming shot and prepare accordingly.

The skills used to analyze the oncoming ball are called *receiving skills* and are often overlooked by beginning players. Your senses can absorb a lot of information, send it to the brain, and transmit a message to your muscles to move. Experience in receiving a ball may come from other sport experiences or from rallying with a partner on the tennis court. Don't discount it as a key skill or you will never be in the best position to strike the ball. The best position to play the shot is one in which your body is under control, balanced, and at a comfortable distance from the ball. If the ball is likely to land a good distance from you, sprint into position with full strides but, as you get near to the ball, switch to small steps to help you adjust to the bounce of the ball. Hold your racket comfortably above your waist and keep your knees flexed as you approach the ball.

Once you have judged the oncoming ball, move with dynamic balance to the spot you've chosen for making your shot. You'd like your body to be under control even while moving. Most of us can achieve pretty good body balance while standing in a static position. In a dynamic situation, such as

Early preparation helps ensure an effective shot.

when you are moving into position or chasing down an opponent's shot, body balance is more of a challenge. The key is to maintain balance, a low center of gravity, and a relaxed upper body to strike the ball.

Swing the Racket

Prepare the racket with a unit turn by rotating your shoulders, hips, and racket together, with your feet pointed straight ahead toward the incoming ball (figure 6.2). This prevents rotating too far. If your racket is in a comfortable position just in front of your body and above the height of the net, you are ready to play any ball.

Many players first learn to hit a tennis ball by taking the racket back to prepare to play a shot. Surprisingly, in doubles play, you almost never have to take the racket back. In fact, if you are in the habit of taking your racket back, you need to learn a new habit, the unit turn.

Figure 6.2 **Unit turn of shoulders, hips, and racket.**

Many excellent doubles players get along just fine by taking short, abbreviated backswings and moving quickly into a net position, which is not a place for taking your racket back. In fact, the closer you are to the net, the time and need for a backswing drops to zero.

Think of it this way: When you are behind the baseline, a backswing helps you generate racket head speed to propel the ball a distance of 75 feet (22.9 meters) to land inside the baseline. As you move forward into the court, your shots have less distance to travel and need to have less power applied. Further, the time you have to react to the oncoming shot is reduced, which means there is no time for a lengthy backswing.

One way to remember this is to think of the backswing you use from behind the baseline as a five on a scale of zero to five (figure 6.3). At the end of a backswing from the baseline area, your racket will point to the back fence as you take a full swing. As you move toward the net, the numbers go down, so that once you close in to the net, the backswing needed is a zero. From the midcourt, most shots would be labeled a three.

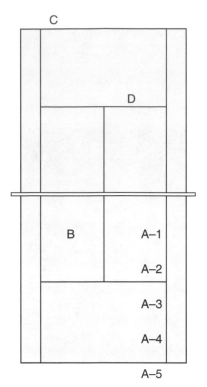

Figure 6.3 Swing size depending on court position.

The next time you are late preparing for a shot or your shot lands well long on the other side, check the length of your backswing. Did it correspond to your court position? Here are the situations in which it makes no sense to take a backswing:

- At the net when playing a hard, oncoming shot or even an easy one from an opponent who is at the net
- In the midcourt when you are the receiver's partner and your opponent volleys the ball at you from the net
- In the midcourt if you are running forward to scrape up a short shot or a sharp angle
- In the midcourt if you are hitting an approach shot off the bounce or out of the air
- At the baseline when your opponent hits a fast, well-placed serve
- At the baseline when you are hitting a defensive lob
- Anyplace where you are trying to return an overhead smash

You might be bold enough then to wonder when you should take a backswing in doubles. Here is the answer. Take a backswing when you are driving the ball from near the baseline and want to apply power and spin to the ball. That is about it for good doubles.

Time the Impact of the Ball and Racket

Timing the impact of the ball and racket is a striking skill that requires eye–hand coordination. Happily, once we have developed eye–hand coordination as children, there is little deterioration even at advanced ages. When playing tennis, your concern is timing the collision of the racket with the ball in your hitting zone. Your hitting zone should be a comfortable distance from your body, a distance that allows you to swing freely. Typically, contact with the ball is made even with or slightly in front of the forward foot.

To increase your chances of hitting a good shot, move your racket forward through the hitting zone by imagining hitting several balls in a row lined up one behind the other (figure 6.4). During your swing, you want to hit each ball by moving your racket straight along the path of the shot. Your racket head should move in the direction of the intended flight of the ball to your target. If you change the direction of your racket face too soon, it won't feel like a solid shot.

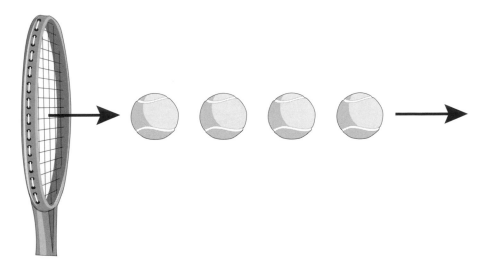

Figure 6.4   Racket path: hitting four balls in succession.

STROKE DOCTOR

Maintain a *quiet racket face* from the beginning of your swing through the finish. No movements, twists, turns, or flips are allowed. If you think of it as *presenting the racket face (strings) to the oncoming ball*, your wrist will be in the optimum position at contact.

Another helpful way of imagining a quiet racket face is to think about balancing a penny on the edge of your racket. If the penny falls off during the swing, your racket face was not in the right spot consistently.

Finish the Shot and Recover

The follow-through is important for allowing your racket arm to slow after impact with the ball. The size of the follow-through should be directly related to the size and speed of the swing: A large, fast swing requires a longer follow-through, and a short swing usually produces a short follow-through. Along with allowing your racket arm to slow gradually, a good follow-through also ensures that you will move your racket smoothly through the path to hit the ball and apply spin to control your shot.

The direction of the follow-through on most shots is toward your target on the other side of the net. However, when you generate a lot of power by rotating the hips and trunk, the follow-through often ends naturally on the opposite side of your body. This typically happens on the serve or an overhead smash or after a powerful forehand drive.

If you have maintained your balance throughout the swing, your recovery for the next shot will be much easier. As soon as you have completed the follow-through, regain your balance and prepare to move into position for the next shot.

Control the Body

Because tennis is a racket sport, the racket often gets too much credit for both excellent and lousy shots. Your job is to control your body to allow the racket to do the racket work.

Body balance is best when your feet are comfortably spread to about shoulder width and your upper body is erect. Too many players believe they should bend from the waist to reach low balls, but it is far more efficient and effective to bend the knees to adjust your body height. If you bend from the waist rather than your knees, your rear end will stick out unflatteringly, your body will be off balance, and your shot is more likely to pop up weakly. If bending your knees is difficult because of injury or age, make every effort to reach the ball at a higher point by moving forward to play it out of the air at waist height.

Think of a plumb line that extends from the top of your head down through your spine and keep that in place throughout a shot. When you actually play a shot, use the nonracket arm for balance to offset the swing of the racket arm. The nonracket arm should not dangle loosely while the other arm swings the racket. Instead use your nonracket arm to help turn your shoulders during the backswing, and then counterbalance your body rotation during the swing. The nonracket arm can be an effective balancing mechanism during ground strokes, serves, volleys, and overhead smashes.

Good balance with a still head ensures a solid shot.

Distribute your body weight by keeping your feet about shoulder-width apart. You can move faster and more efficiently if you keep your weight on the balls of your feet rather than on your heels. As you run for a ball, push off with your toes and plant your foot first with the toe and then the heels. A flatfooted landing will jar your entire body and prevent quick movements.

Use a split-step or check-step as you move around the court. This is a hesitation that allows you to reclaim body balance and is much like a hopscotch landing on both feet. The timing of the split-step is critical. It should be done just as your opponent is about to swing at the ball. The momentary pause in your movement helps you recover balance and change direction to move forward, right, left, or backward. Without a check-step, your body will be out of control, and you will have to scramble to chase a lot of shots. Even if you never get to play a ball during a point, you should make a split-step every time one of your opponents is about to strike the ball.

Muscle tension can interfere with a smooth swing, especially if you are nervous or excited to hit a ball. Make every effort to breathe naturally (some players unintentionally hold their breath during each shot) and relax your muscles throughout the shot. Tense muscles will restrict your shot and usually affect your timing of the hit or restrict the follow-through and recovery after the shot. On touch shots such as a drop, drop volley, or lob volley, tension in the upper body will ruin the shot for sure.

Many inexperienced tennis players hold the racket tightly while in the waiting position. Some players do this to be sure they have the correct grip, and others do it because they are anxious about the next point. It is far better to hold the racket at the throat with the nonracket hand and gently at the handle with your racket hand. Imagine you are holding a newborn baby, your child, or grandchild. You would hold her firmly but gently; treat your racket the same.

Moving your head during the swing is a common problem in tennis. Golfers and baseball players endure the same challenge. Often players move the head to look up to see the great shot they've just hit. Sometimes, players raise their heads in response to an opponent who is moving just as they're hitting their shot. Head movement during the swing will cause you to take your eye off the ball at the point of contact, which is just when you need it most. You'll also probably lift your head too quickly, preventing you from completing the swing through the hitting area. Resist the temptation and keep your head still until well into your follow-through.

Ball Control

Although there are various ways to describe how to control your shots, we have found the following terms the most effective for the majority of players:

- *Height* is controlled by opening or closing the face of the racket.
- *Direction* is controlled by aiming the racket face to the right, left, or center at the moment of contact.
- *Speed* is controlled by the size and speed of your swing. To hit a ball gently, abbreviate your backswing and move the racket slowly toward contact. To increase the speed of your shot, take a larger swing to build racket momentum and build up speed to the moment of contact.

- *Depth* or *distance* is controlled by a combination of the height of the ball over the net and the amount of spin you apply to the shot.
- *Spin* controls the flight of the ball and affects its bounce.

You can apply just three types of spin to a tennis ball: topspin, backspin, and sidespin. (Figure 6.5 shows the effects of topspin and backspin.) Each type of spin can be useful for certain shots. Backspin can be used for slice returns of serve, volleys, lobs, and drop shots. Usually topspin is used only on forehand or backhand drives, serves, and sometimes on lobs. Sidespin is often used for slice serves and occasionally on approach shots or reaction volleys.

Topspin causes the ball to rotate in the direction it is traveling. Balls with topspin typically dip during flight and bounce higher when they contact the ground than shots with backspin do. To put topspin on the ball, move the racket face from low to high to brush the back of the ball (figure 6.6, *a* and *b*).

Backspin causes the ball to rotate back toward the hitter. Balls with backspin tend to float a bit more when hit from the baseline. When you play a volley from the net with backspin, the downward trajectory and spin cause it to skid and stay low after the bounce. To apply backspin to the ball (figure 6.7, *a* and *b*), keep the racket face slightly open. The bottom edge of the racket's strings should hit the ball first. The forward swing of the racket should begin slightly higher than where the point of impact with the ball will occur.

Sidespin causes the ball to rotate sideways and curve in an arc. Balls with sidespin curve in flight and may be effective, especially if you slice the serve. Sidespin is rarely used on ground strokes or volleys except when defending yourself with a backhand volley hit right at you or sometimes when hitting an approach shot on the way to the net. Sidespin is often used

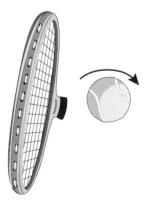

Topspin: ball rotates forward

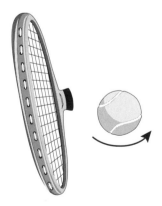

Backspin: ball rotates backward

Figure 6.5 **Effect of topspin and backspin.**

a   b

Figure 6.6   **Applying topspin to the ball.**

a   b

Figure 6.7   **Applying backspin to the ball.**

unintentionally. To apply sidespin to the ball, drag the racket face across the side of the ball. In general, we do not suggest using sidespin on ground strokes or volleys. Usually sidespin is used only by accident. This is one shot probably not worth practicing.

STROKE DOCTOR

To get more spin, exaggerate the upward or downward motion. To get less spin, flatten the swing.

Spin controls the distance of the shot, takes the pace off a shot for control, and produces a predictable ball flight. On the other hand, excessive spin can fool an opponent by providing a more complicated reception of the ball.

Shotmaking Errors

In tennis, most points are won because a player makes an error while hitting a shot. It is far more rare to win a point with an outright placement that is out of your opponent's reach. Let's look at the types of errors that are typically made and how you can reduce the number of points that you allow your opponents to win with no effort.

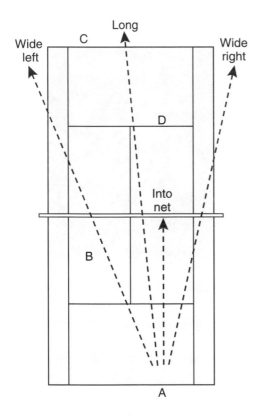

Figure 6.8 **Four types of errors.**

Types of Errors

The four types of shotmaking errors are hitting the ball into the net, hitting it wide right of the sideline, hitting it wide left of the sideline, and hitting it long beyond the baseline (figure 6.8).

Errors into the net are the most embarrassing. The net is the first barrier your shot must clear, so aim most of your shots safely over the net. If your shot doesn't go over the net at exactly the height you planned, err by hitting it just a bit higher than you planned. Because your opponents are often at the net position, the temptation is to hit the perfect shot that just clears the net. The folly in this strategy is that if you miscalculate even a small amount, you lose the point outright.

Eliminate most errors outside the sideline by aiming for the singles sideline or down the middle of the court. That margin for error will ensure that even a sharply angled shot will land in the court most of the time. Go back to chapters 4 and 5 on strategy to see where the typical targets are for doubles shots. You'll notice they are safely inside the sidelines and baseline.

In an earlier section, we explained that the racket face at contact controlled the side-to-side direction of the shot. Sometimes a timing error sends the ball to the left or right. A right-handed player who times the swing a bit early will likely cause the ball to go to the left. A right-handed player who swings a bit late will likely cause the ball to go to the right. Time your swing by thinking early or late to gain better control of the direction of your shots.

Reduce the number of errant shots that land long over the baseline by applying more spin to control the distance of the shot, and make sure your backswing is the appropriate length to play a ball in the midcourt or at the net.

Forced or Unforced Errors

Tennis announcers on television like to keep track of player errors by labeling them as *forced* or *unforced*. The difference between the two types is whether your opponents caused you to make an error or you did it all by yourself. Focus more on the errors you make without provocation and reduce their frequency. If your opponents force you to make an error through a brilliant shot, good sporting behavior requires that you simply compliment her on a fine shot and move on to the next point.

As you analyze your errors, first determine whether they are a result of poor shot choice or poor execution of the right shot. If you have absorbed the strategic principles of doubles play, you should recognize the best-percentage shot depending on where you are in the court and where your opponents are. You should also know which of your shots are strengths and which are weaknesses. As the match progresses, you will also gather information on the strengths and weaknesses of your opponents. After a shot that proves to be an error, quickly evaluate whether it was the best choice of shot to play. If it was not, when that situation presents itself again, try a higher-percentage shot.

Often players choose the right shot but simply execute it poorly. In that case, evaluate your preparation for the shot, your racket work, and body work. Perhaps you need to adjust the speed or spin of your shot, adjust your target, or learn to keep your head steady throughout the shot. Over time, you will begin to see patterns of errors in execution. These errors may need to be corrected by taking a lesson or just practicing between match play with a partner.

THE CASE OF STEADY EDDIE

Nobody at the tennis club could figure out how Steady Eddie ended up in the club doubles championships year after year. He even accomplished it with three different partners. He never seemed to inspire others with his shotmaking ability, but he nearly always was on the winning team. A group of club members decided to take the case and ferret out his secret.

Careful observation revealed a few clear patterns. Eddie rarely missed a first serve, preferring to hit it at about 75 percent speed with plenty of spin. His second serve was almost the same, but hit with more spin. When he was on the receiving team, Eddie used drives, chips, and lobs. What was most impressive, however, was that he hardly ever missed a return.

Eddie was not young, pushing 70, and he didn't seem to run that well. But rarely was he ever out of position. When his fellow club members watched him throughout a point, they figured out why. When the ball was on the other side of the net, Eddie worked hard to get into a prime position.

One other thing the club members noticed. When his opponents hit the ball hard to him, Eddie took speed off the ball by shortening his swing and adding more spin. As his opponents tried to hit harder to force an error, he stayed calm and unhurried, happy to make them hit one more shot.

Some people, with a hint of disdain, said Eddie was just a steady player. But Eddie had a mantle full of club trophies and a line of potential partners for next year's championship.

All-Purpose Doubles Shot

If you want to learn just one shot that you can use in almost every situation during a doubles point, learn a sliced shot. For purposes of this discussion, we've defined a slice shot as any shot hit with backspin. Backspin shots include slices, chips, and lobs from the baseline; approach shots and drop shots at midcourt; and volleys and lob volleys at the net. It is critical in doubles play because you play lots of balls from the midcourt and up at the net where slice is used almost exclusively. The slice (figure 6.9, a-c) is the most flexible, adaptable shot with little risk of error. We'll explain why.

Slice at the Net

Let's start at the net because that is the best position in doubles play. Volleys should be hit with a short backswing and a relatively short punching motion. The key to applying spin is to lead with the lower edge of the racket face to produce backspin on the ball. Keep your wrist relatively firm and

a
b
c

Figure 6.9 The slice shot is the all-purpose doubles shot. The key is to lead with the lower edge of the racket as you contact the ball.

slightly laid back to produce consistency at the contact point. Finish the shot in the direction of the intended flight of the ball and use about the same length as the backswing. For example, if the backswing is 12 inches, the forward swing is also 12 inches.

If, as the receiver's partner, you are forced to play a ball volleyed aggressively at you, execute a reflex volley by simply presenting your racket face to the ball and using the speed from your opponent's shot. An alternative shot is the lob volley. Execute the lob volley by opening the racket face and lifting the ball with backspin over your opponent's reach.

Slice at Midcourt

Midcourt shots will happen often, and a sliced shot is the best choice. If you play the ball out of the air or after the bounce, the technique is the same. Use a medium-size (three out of five) backswing, lead with the lower edge of the racket, and use a flat swing to hit the ball deep in your opponents' court. If you want to hit a short angle against an opponent at the baseline, shorten the backswing to a two and hit more downward to produce more spin and less depth on your shot.

Another time to use backspin is when you are running forward to reach a low ball and the only way to play it is with an open racket face to get it over the net. Again, backspin will help you control the length.

One other shot that can be hit from midcourt is the drop shot. Although some coaches tell players not to use this shot in doubles on soft, clay courts against older opponents, this shot is a killer if you don't overdo it. If your opponent hangs out at the baseline, it is likely because she doesn't feel comfortable at the net. Invite her up to the net with a delicate drop shot. Open your racket face, soften your hands, and slide your racket under the ball to produce excessive backspin. Aim for a foot or two (30 to 60 centimeters) over the net to allow a margin of safety.

The main ingredient to a successful drop shot is disguise. When you prepare to hit the shot, use a short unit turn that looks the same as any other shot so that your opponents do not know which shot you are going to hit.

Practice Tip

Drop shots and short angled shots from inside the service line are easy and fun to practice. Practice short shots with your partner during the warm-up or make a competitive game of it by requiring every shot to land in the service boxes and only playing balls on the bounce. These tennis skills come in handy during a frantic point.

Slice From the Baseline

At the baseline, a sliced ball with backspin can be an effective return of serve. Sometimes these shots are called a *chop* or a *chip*. The common trait in these shots is backspin. The difference is the amount of downward motion. If you are trying to land the ball over the net but at the feet of the oncoming player, a short, chopping motion will keep the ball short. Conversely, if you are trying to send the ball deep, use a longer swing in a flat path to apply less spin and achieve greater depth.

The final shot with backspin is a lob from the baseline. Most players assume you just open the racket face to lob, but applying spin is the key to controlling distance. Especially if you are returning an opponent's overhead smash, lead with the lower edge of the racket face as you push the racket slowly upward. You'll see the magic of spin as your lob lands right back in the court.

So there is your all-purpose doubles shot—a slice hit with backspin. The shot varies depending on your position in the court and your objective, but the variations look pretty much the same. Slice, dink, chip, and chop are all used to describe these wonderful shots.

Topspin Drive

You may wonder, "When do I get to hit my topspin shots?" Topspin is the better choice in the following situations:

- You can drive a ball aggressively from the baseline.
- You are trying to pass the net players outright by using speed.
- You are trying to dip the ball at the net player's feet and force him to volley up.
- You are pushed behind the baseline but are in a good, balanced position to execute a topspin lob. If you get it over the head of an opponent, it will bounce away from him and probably be an outright winner. This shot works best when your opponents are hugging in toward the net.

If you want to be a complete doubles player, you need to hit all the spins and know which one makes the most sense in each situation. You may find some shots easier to execute than others because of your past experience, grips, swings, and preferences. Try to make smart shot choices and challenge yourself to add new shots. A new shot is just another arrow in your quiver.

Touch Shots

Over years of play, you will encounter players who have mastered certain specialty shots in doubles. Most of these shots are touch shots, such as a drop volley, half-volley, or lob volley. These shots rarely occur in singles play, which is played more from the baseline. They have in common a requirement of soft hands, which means you absorb some of the shock of the ball hitting your racket. How is this done?

Suppose someone threw a fresh egg in your direction. If you wanted to catch it without breaking it, how would you do it? The secret is to relax your hands, absorb the impact of the egg, and give way with your body. Soft, delicate shots in tennis require much the same technique. You have to have a relaxed upper body and arm and think of feathering the shot with your racket. No backswing is required because you are trying to reduce the speed of the ball, but you must use a slow follow-through to ensure spin and control of direction. The sensation for these shots is more of a catch and push than a hit.

Overhead Smash

The overhead smash represents the best of times and the worst of times. This specialty shot can result in a satisfying winning shot or an embarrassing, humiliating miss. The following are key technique suggestions for successful overhead smashes.

Getting into position quickly is the first order of business to prepare for the shot. Anticipate where you need to move and get your body sideways to the oncoming ball. Next, lift both arms to prepare to hit the shot. The racket arm should move quickly upward with a short backswing. Raise the nonracket arm for balance.

During the hitting phase of the shot, bend your racket arm with a relaxed swing, just like on the serve, and swing up to the ball. Time the descent of the ball so that you hit it at the highest point you can reach comfortably. The moment of truth is the contact point with the ball.

Contact the ball about a foot (30 centimeters) in front of your body so that your racket face points down at the court. (This is different from the contact point for the serve, where the flight of the ball off your racket must be upward or the ball will land in the net because of the pull of gravity.) Resist the temptation to try to hit the ball down into the court. Rather, let your racket face do that job by making contact out in front and pointing your racket strings down. Above all, keep your head steady and look up toward the contact point throughout the swing.

To finish the shot, follow through with your racket arm as it decelerates and moves diagonally across your body just like it does in the serving motion. At this point you should quickly recover into your ready position in case your opponent is able to return your smash and you have to play another shot.

Practicing Doubles Skills

We would like to share a little theory of practice so that you and your partner can practice between matches. It can be fun and a great workout. The following are ideas that we guarantee will improve your doubles skills.

Blocked and Random Trials

Use both blocked and random trials to practice skills. This advice borrows a principle from the science of learning sport skills: Use the blocked method of practice when first learning a skill until you can perform the skill successfully, and then switch to the random method of practice to set the habit so that it will work in a playing situation.

When you first learn a new skill, you need multiple repetitions to establish the motor patterns, refine them, and overlearn them so that you retain them. This kind of practice, in which you concentrate solely on one skill, is called *blocked*. Through it, you can become proficient hitting multiple shots and seem ready for match play.

Suppose you want to improve your forehand volley. Your partner feeds you repetitive volleys and you start by focusing on your technique. After some success, you move on to volleying to different targets. After a while you think you're ready to use your newly improved volley in match play. But alas, as soon as you play a match, the same old mistakes appear.

Unfortunately, in match play, you usually don't get to hit the same shot repeatedly. Instead, you might have to hit a serve, a first volley from the service line, and a second volley closer to the net and then finish the point with an overhead smash. Shots tend to occur in patterns, but they can also be totally random depending on your opponents.

To be truly prepared, you must practice the skills that tend to occur together in sequence and expect randomness depending on your opponent's choice of shot. Have your practice partner mix it up so that you can practice a particular shot in combination with other shots without knowing which to expect. *Random practice* will sharpen your decision-making skills and test your ability to adjust instantly to an opponent's shot.

When you take a lesson from a teaching professional, expect a blocked approach at first. But be sure to finish your session with random practice to test your new skill in a more realistic playing situation. If you are practicing on your own with a partner, follow the same approach by using a blocked approach first and then test your skill with random practice.

One-on-One Doubles

Play one-on-one doubles in practice. You and your partner can easily practice doubles skills by playing out points cross-court. A ball that lands on the other side of the center service line is out (figure 6.10). From this formation, you can practice serve and return. First serve and volley. Then serve and play out the point. The receiver can mix up different types of returns, passing shots, and lobs.

We like to do this with one player serving until someone earns 10 points. Then we switch serves. If you are losing your service games, it becomes very clear that you cannot blame your partner.

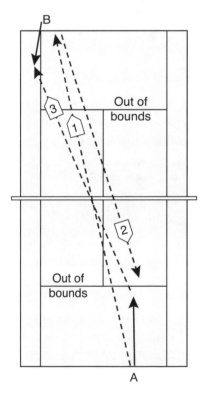

Figure 6.10 **One-on-one doubles.**

Two Steps Up or Three Back

Use half of the court straight ahead for this drill. Your partner is at the starting net position and feeds a ball to you at the baseline (figure 6.11).

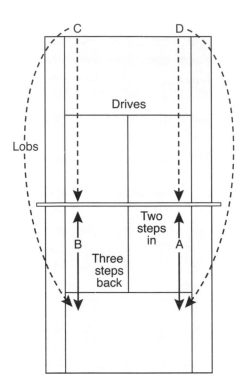

Your choice is to drive or lob. Don't even think about making an error. Your sole objective is to be steady and make your partner move forward and back.

The challenge for the net player (your partner) is to recognize a drive and close in two steps before she plays a volley. If you lob, she has to turn sideways and retreat three steps before she plays an overhead smash. The ball should stay in play for several shots because each of you has a relatively small area to defend and few angles to contend with. This is a great workout and encourages consistency from the baseline player and quick anticipation and footwork from the net player.

Play until one player earns 10 points and then switch roles. An excellent variation of this drill is to play it crosscourt rather than straight ahead. This crosscourt game is closer to the actual game situation of doubles play.

Figure 6.11 Two steps up or three back.

Skill Level Variation

Play against teams of different skill levels. One of our pet peeves is players who claim they can only improve or play well against better players. Well, if that were true (which it is not), whom would the top professional teams play against?

Schedule and play matches against all three types of teams: those clearly a level up, those who are at about the same level so either team could win, and those who are clearly at a lower level. The following are suggestions for playing each of the three levels.

Playing up: Resolve to play consistent, solid tennis to give your team the best chance to compete. If your opponents have an off day, the match may be close and, at the very least, they will enjoy the challenge and invite you to play again. Don't try to play shots you haven't mastered to keep up with your opponents. You'll just make errors sooner and lose more quickly.

Even match: Because the outcome is in doubt, give yourself every chance to win the match. Be smart, play percentage tennis, and work hard as a team. Focus on your match toughness, competitiveness, and ability to handle pressure. Read chapter 3 on mental toughness for specific suggestions.

Playing down: This is a great opportunity for your team to practice certain shots, patterns of play, and formations that you would be reluctant to risk in an even match. Try to poach, serve and volley, and chip and charge or work in other skills that are not part of your everyday game. Play to your opponents' strengths to add to your challenge. We don't suggest that you carry this advice to an extreme and lose the match, but sprinkle in riskier shots and moves when you can afford them, and stay in control of the match.

By the way, you know those close matches when you played so well against stronger teams. Did you realize they were using your team to practice their weaknesses?

WORDS TO THE WISE

- Evaluate your tennis skills, including your preparation, racket technique, and body control.
- Experiment with the five controls of the tennis ball: height, direction, speed, depth or distance, and spin.
- Determine whether the errors you make are errors of shot selection or errors of execution, and correct them.
- Consider adding a dependable slice shot on both the forehand and backhand sides along with a few new doubles specialty shots.
- Practice your doubles skills efficiently with a partner or, better yet, join a group practice.

Mixed Doubles (Avoiding Troubles)

Mixed doubles is a terrific game and one of the few sporting opportunities for men and women to compete directly with and against each other. Yet mixed doubles can also be troublesome, even for couples that get along famously off the tennis court.

In this chapter, we aim to expose the real differences between mixed doubles and doubles played by teams of the same gender. We follow that up with specific advice that will improve your performance in mixed doubles and keep your relationships sane. Here are the specific topics we will cover:

- Tennis: a skill sport, regardless of gender
- Physical advantages of males and their effect on play
- Identifying the game you are playing: social or competitive mixed doubles
- Strategies for social mixed doubles
- Strategies for competitive mixed doubles
- Emotional control strategies

Mixed doubles is unique among sports.

Over several decades of playing with and teaching mixed doubles teams, we've encountered stories of male–female problems that are universal. The She Said, He Said vignettes that appear in this chapter are normal perplexing situations that threaten healthy mixed teams. If any of these symptoms of trouble sound familiar to you, read the strategies for both social and competitive mixed doubles carefully and discuss them candidly with your partner.

Tennis: a Skill Sport

The four dimensions of tennis are racket skill, strategic plan, emotional control, and physical ability. In three of these areas, males and females have equivalent possibilities. It is only in the dimension of raw physical talent that males typically have the edge, and that is not always the case.

In fact, when four people (regardless of gender) take the court to play doubles, there are usually differences in each of the four dimensions between the players. Some players are more skilled in racket work, some are more physically talented, and the best competitors we know are strategically and emotionally a cut above their peers.

Any experienced tennis player knows that players who have a higher degree of racket skill usually dominate play. They have more shot options and can produce the same shots consistently. Provided their strategic plan is sound and emotions are under control, they will win matches more often than not.

So if you plan to play mixed doubles, evaluate the relative strengths and weaknesses of all four players in each of the four dimensions. If the foursome is to be competitive or at least compatible, they should be at similar levels overall even if there are inequities in one dimension.

Competitive mixed doubles players are rated according to the National Tennis Rating Program (NTRP). There are two level comparisons of note between male and female players. According to the NTRP, a male player rated at the 3.5 level is compatible with a female player rated at 4.0. At the higher skill levels, a male player rated 5.0 is compatible with a female at 6.0. These competitive ratings are based on observations of hundreds of thousands of players over the years.

The NTRP ratings are based primarily on racket skills and playing ability and do not take into account the typical physical advantages males have over females in size, strength, power, and explosiveness. The bottom line is that if a male and female are both rated at the 3.0 level, the male player probably will play at a higher level.

Physical Advantages of Male Players

In general, male players are taller and heavier than females. They also usually are stronger and can generate more power. Males also can move a bit faster to cover more court area, and that fact is enhanced by a longer reach.

That said, males have no inherent physical advantages in eye–hand coordination, touch, balance, flexibility, eyesight, tracking a ball, or striking a ball. In addition, females may have better overall endurance over the course of a match and may have a higher level of physical fitness than a male partner.

Since the passage of Title IX in 1972, which assured women and girls equal opportunities to compete in sports in schools, females have flocked to playing fields and tennis courts to join their male counterparts in sports. At the elite level of play, women have proved that they can compete at levels formerly thought attainable only by male athletes.

Let's look at a few salient examples of the achievements of women in sport. In the Olympic Games, Joan Benoit Samuelson's time for the marathon in Los Angeles in 1984 was faster than all men's times in history before 1956. In Olympic swimming, the women's record in the 100-meter freestyle, set in 1992, was faster than all the men's times before 1964. And Billie Jean King defeated Bobby Riggs in the Houston Astrodome before a nationwide television audience in a best-of-five-sets match in 1973.

We now have females in high school and college who can dunk a basketball in a game. Do you have friends or even acquaintances who have dunked a basketball? The point is, even though males have physiological advantages generally, the differences are no longer as great as they used to be. When you play mixed doubles, don't automatically assume the females will be the weaker players on the court.

A typical problem arises in mixed play when a male player of modest tennis skill and understanding has the physical ability to hit the ball powerfully but with little control. If "Slugging Sammy" catches a ball just right and decks the opponent or even his partner with an errant serve, nobody will be happy. This situation can be dangerous for everyone on the court and requires that every player be on full alert throughout the match. And your friend Sammy may want to work on controlling his shots at about three-fourths speed and save the power display for another day.

© Associated Press

Billie Jean King raises her hands in victory over Bobby Riggs, proving women can compete with men.

Identify the Game:
Social or Competitive Mixed Doubles

Social mixed doubles is typically played by four people who want to spend time together socially in a fun physical activity that they all enjoy. The focus is not on the outcome of the match, but rather the enjoyment of testing their overall skills as mixed doubles teams.

Hundreds of thousands of players love to play mixed doubles with friends or in club mixed doubles events and enjoy a social hour with food and drink afterward. It's a great way to spend time with people you care about or enjoy spending time with in your favorite sport. And it sure beats riding a stationary bicycle or walking on a treadmill for exercise.

The only risk in social mixed doubles pops up if one of the players (or more) thinks he or she is playing competitive doubles. Here's where the situation can become tense between either partners or opponents. Clarification beforehand can help prevent this unpleasant state of affairs. If you do get in a situation like this, a few well-chosen remarks may be necessary to remind everyone that you're playing for fun, not blood.

In social mixed doubles, all four players celebrate a great shot.

Competitive mixed doubles is no different from the doubles games we've described in other chapters. There is a keen interest in the outcome of the match, although it won't help anyone to focus on that fact. All four players have accepted the challenge of competing to see which team will finish first that day and which team will earn second place.

Decisions in competitive mixed doubles should be made according to how they might affect your team's chance of winning the match. If hitting to the weaker player seems to be a smart strategy, you can certainly go for it.

So you and your partner have to decide whether you're looking for a social or competitive game of mixed doubles. If you can't agree, we predict that trouble will result. You also need to find opponents who are looking for the same game. Be careful of mixed doubles events that send mixed messages. They may advertise fun and sociability, but when you arrive you find out match scores are recorded, prizes are awarded to winners, and the results will be published in the club newsletter. In this case, a comfortable game of social mixed doubles may suddenly shift to the competitive arena.

SHE SAID, HE SAID

She: I get so intimidated playing social doubles with my spouse. He acts like my boss, telling me where to play and how to hit shots, and he doesn't know what he is talking about. Just because he can hit harder and is faster covering the court, he expects me to stand by and watch him play. I want to play doubles the right way. During lessons with the club professional, she helps us with strategy and shot selection that is right for us. My spouse sure doesn't want to take directions from me, even if I'm right.

He: What a drag to play mixed. After hundreds of hours of tennis clinics I've paid for, my wife thinks she is a coach. I like to play on instinct and athleticism like I play other sports, but "Ms. Coach" has other ideas. I don't enjoy playing like she does with the girls. To me, it makes more sense to do what works and gives us the best chance of winning. Are we doomed as a team?

Both players in the She Said, He Said situation need to reassess their reasons for playing mixed doubles, and once they agree, work out strategies that are acceptable to both of them. Both players have to be willing to compromise in order to find a balance that will satisfy both. Perhaps some of the guidelines in this chapter will help.

Strategies for Social Mixed Doubles

Here are strategies to consider when playing social mixed doubles:

- Allow the weaker player to choose the side of the court for receiving serve to maximize the chance of points starting off with a ball in play.
- Either player may begin serving the set. Taking turns serving first is probably a good idea.
- All players should agree that they will not smash or volley balls with pace directly at an opponent who is uncomfortable on defense.

The stronger players should do the following:

- Aim winning shots for an open area of the court or at least at an aim point on the ground, never at a person's body.
- Rarely hit powerful ground strokes with pace and never aim them at a net player who is uneasy playing there.
- Set up some points so that the stronger partners exchange shots with each other and try to win the point.
- Encourage partners to cover their fair share of the court and coach them to bisect the angles of possible returns. If the stronger players put their partners near the alleys and then they play the majority of shots, they are essentially removing their partners from the play. What fun is that?
- Hit most shots at about three-fourths speed and keep the ball in play for several shots so that all four players can enjoy the excitement of an exchange. All professional players and coaches become quite skilled at this and call it *customer tennis*. If you are the better player, why not act like a pro, at least for that match?
- Help their partners by calling lines whenever possible and clearly call who should play balls when there may be indecision.

The weaker players should do the following:

- Play from their strengths. If they feel more comfortable playing from the baseline, it's okay to do so except when their partners are serving.
- Cover their fair share of the court and don't expect their partners to cover everything.
- Aim to keep balls in play so that everyone can enjoy a good exchange. Aim high enough over the net so that unforced errors into the net do not cut rallies short.

- Hit most shots down the middle to reduce errors and perhaps cause confusion between the opponents.
- Review the differences between inside and outside balls as presented in chapter 3, and play them accordingly.
- Be extra ready and alert to play oncoming shots that they may not be used to seeing with pace, spin, or placement.
- Take chances at the net, especially when their partner is serving. If the speed of the ball is intimidating, move back a step or two to allow more time to react. Keep their racket in front of the body, resist the temptation to take the racket back, and defend their body with their backhand from head to knees.
- Try to get the first serve in the court to reduce the pressure of having to deliver a second serve.
- Aim most shots to the weaker player on the other team whenever possible.

Let's close this discussion of social mixed doubles with a suggestion that has worked well for us. We prefer matches of four games, especially in mixed doubles mixers or move-up doubles in which the objective is to play against multiple teams during the event.

During any game, if the score reaches deuce, play one point to decide the game. On this point, if a male is serving, he must serve to the male on the other side of the net to the service court where the male has been playing. Further, if the overall score becomes tied at two games all, play one tiebreak point to determine the winning team, again using a male-to-male or female-to-female arrangement for serving and receiving. Before the one-point tiebreak, spin the racket. The winning team chooses to serve or receive serve. The serving team gets to choose which partner will serve, thereby locking in the receiving team to a receiver of the same gender. This insignificant rule change protects both males and females from uncomfortable situations and can provide intriguing strategic maneuvering.

Strategies for Competitive Mixed Doubles

The objective of competitive mixed doubles is to play the best you can on that day and give your team the best opportunity to win the match. We suggest you reread chapters 4 and 5 on doubles strategy and work as a team to implement those principles. Regardless of gender, the game of angles and percentages is the same.

The situation described in the He Said, She Said sidebar shows both sides of a common situation in which the male player prefers to play doubles

HE SAID, SHE SAID

He: I love to play at the net, but my partner constantly hangs back at the baseline. I've seen her volley quite well when we practice, but during a match she actually sometimes runs backward to retreat to the baseline. How can I get her to come up to the net with me when we have the offensive opportunity?

She: I don't mind playing at the net in ladies doubles, but against some of the men we play, it's just suicide. They drive the ball so hard right at the net player that I fear for my life. When I do venture in, it never fails that my partner gives them a ball they can punish right at me. How can I get it through his head that I am not comfortable at the net?

at the net, and his partner is more comfortable at the baseline, especially against a male opponent.

We've heard this conversation many times. Most female players are simply not used to the speed or spin that some male opponents put on the ball. The only solution is to build confidence and skill gradually in practice by practicing against hard-hit balls until they feel comfortable. In most cases, it is a matter of technique and experience rather than lack of ability. After all, you only have to deflect the ball at the net to protect yourself, and often that shot will be a winning one. But it does take training and repetition to keep from using backswing on reflex volleys.

Another suggestion is to position the female player a few steps farther from the net to gain an extra second of time to receive a hard hit. The trade-off she'll have to make is accepting that she will need to be skilled at making low volleys from her shoe tops. Again, no backswing and a slightly open racket face on low volleys will do the trick.

A third suggestion is for the male partner to play volleys or short balls aggressively to drive the opposing team back. From behind the baseline, their drives will be less intimidating, or they will lob. If the female partner at the net is constantly bombarded with laser drives, the male partner can help her out by hitting more aggressively himself.

Let's take a look at other strategic situations that arise in competitive mixed doubles that, although they do occur, are not as typical in same-gender doubles.

- When the male has a strong serve that is difficult to return, the female receiver should shorten her swing and just try to block or lob the ball back. Her partner may want to move back close to the baseline because the team is clearly in a defensive position.

- If one player has a definite preference for hitting either forehands or backhands, set him or her up for that shot by using the Australian formation on one side (see figure 5.4, page 64). You can protect the weaker shot that way.

- If the female player is susceptible to the lob, she may need to back off from the net almost to the service line, particularly if her partner is trying to serve and volley. If she gets lobbed repeatedly, her team will always be on the defensive even when serving.

- Many mixed teams play a lot of points in the one-up, one-back formation with the male at the net. The male net player should cut off any ball above the height of the net that he can reach and should also be alert to covering short shots on the other side of the net that may be out of his partner's reach.

- If the opposing male net player poaches frequently, both players on the opposing team must try shots down the line or try to lob over his head to discourage his constant crossing. A partner should warn the other before doing so to alert him or her to be ready to reflex a volley or give ground when facing an overhead smash.

- If the female partner has a relatively weak serve and the opposing male is hitting aggressive returns, try the Australian or I formation (see figures 5.4 and 5.5, pages 64 and 65) at the net to give him a different look.

- The better server should usually serve first in the set because his or her serve will come up more often. However, don't be deceived just because the male has a stronger serve. A team may actually have more success with the male at the net and the female serving if her serve is dependable and well-placed and lands deep in the service box.

- Test the other team early in the match with lobs to see what happens. Many mixed teams have difficulty covering lobs, and if you lob well and stay alert, you will take the net position from them for easy points.

- If the female player is the better player overall, she should play the lead role and accommodate the strengths and weakness of her partner. That just makes good sense.

Our advice for competitive mixed doubles is to play to win, but still keep in mind our caution about the physical well-being of all players. If you see that your opponents are not fully capable of defending themselves against a blazing overhead smash or sharp volley, aim for the open court or a spot on the court rather than at the body. You'll get no long-term satisfaction from raising a bruise or welt on an unsuspecting opponent, and you may avoid causing a more serious injury.

HE SAID, SHE SAID

He: Mixed doubles isn't much fun for me. I'm always worrying about the opposing female. I don't want to embarrass her or, even worse, injure her. Then I change the shots I normally play and end up costing us the point. I could kick myself for all the easy putaways that I held back. I just don't ever get to play full out like I do with my buddies.

She: I hate to play against men who are so condescending and treat me with kid gloves. I grew up playing against my brothers and father, who never held back against me. In college I played some pretty hard hitters, too, and didn't back off. Believe me, I know when to duck and when to scrap out a point. The most annoying thing is when a male opponent misses an easy sitter and then blames it on me.

Emotional Control Strategies

Any team sport requires that partners or teammates support each other emotionally before, during, and after play. This is a skill that is learned just like the physical skills on the court. In the heat of battle, people sometimes lose emotional balance and say or do things they regret later.

Female player giving her partner "the look."

When you play mixed doubles with a significant other, your interactions are magnified. Even if you say nothing, you may be accused of being insensitive. Add in the cultural differences between men and women, and it can be a recipe for disaster.

Concern, or a lack of it, for a partner's feelings and emotions is especially magnified for married teams. Even looks without words can be upsetting to a sensitive partner. Reassurance and positive feedback are much more powerful than dirty looks or snide comments.

SHE SAID, HE SAID

She: I really love my husband, but we just can't play mixed doubles together. I can't tell you how many times I've ended up in tears, sometimes during the match. It's embarrassing for me and our opponents. If I get upset, he always asks, "What did I say?" Most of the time, it's not what he says but how he says it. Or sometimes he just gives me a look that could kill. I get so nervous playing with him, I'm not the same player I am with the girls. I guess we should just play with different partners if we're going to play mixed.

He: My wife is so sensitive. If I even look at her wrong, she takes offense. She blames every incident on me when her play is the reason we play so badly. She's a wonderful woman off the court, but in competition she just falls to pieces. When I try to encourage her, she shuts me out and tells me to concentrate on my own game. I just don't see why she can't take a few constructive suggestions from me during a match.

The scenario described in the She Said, He Said sidebar is all too common. Perhaps off-court feelings bubble up under the stress of competition. The result is that no one has fun. And the long-term lack of teamwork may extend off the court.

An honest talk after emotions have retreated is in order. Both people have to accept what has happened and identify the behavior that triggers it. To be a successful competitor, you have to be your own best friend. That means no negative self-talk or thoughts. Transfer that advice to a doubles team. You'll notice that even professional players talk and touch frequently. Making eye contact is critical, too. Teammates reinforce effort and good shots every time with a positive comment or a high five. Errors or missed shots are best ignored, but not too many in a row. Comments such as "bad luck," "no worries," or "we'll get the next one" are priceless for a partner who makes a mistake.

You may notice even in the cut-throat world of college basketball competition, teammates touch hands with a teammate before and after they attempt foul shots regardless of whether the shot goes in or not. The gesture simply means, "We're with you and know you are trying your hardest." People don't make mistakes on purpose, even though it sometimes looks like it from the sidelines. When you're in the heat of battle, it looks quite different.

If things aren't going well during a match, take a moment to relax and cool down while changing sides and then propose a change in tactics by saying something like, "I wonder if we would do better playing more balls away from the net player or lobbing?" This gives your partner a chance to agree, take the suggestion, and save face.

It's not easy for anyone to keep emotional control in the heat of competition. It takes skill, training, and practice to become a good sport and a great competitor. Some professional players who have dedicated their whole lives to playing tennis struggle mightily. It's worth investing time and effort into developing your emotional skills. You'll find those skills will also come in handy in other more daunting life situations.

If problems persist in mixed doubles, consider asking for help from an unbiased third party. A mature, experienced coach or teaching professional can quickly spot flaws in your team game plan or execution. As an unbiased third party, she can be objective and moderate disputes. She may be able to point out key phrases to use as cues, for example, prepare earlier, down the middle, racket face to the ball, angle it away, and net clearance. She also can point out how to positively reinforce each other and ignore your partner's mistakes.

If you can find a fourth player, take a playing lesson so that the coach actually plays in your foursome. That's the best way to expose potential trouble spots and receive suggestions for solutions.

WORDS TO THE WISE

- Tennis is a skill sport, regardless of gender. The four dimensions of tennis are racket skill, strategic plan, emotional control, and physical ability.
- Recognize the general physical advantages male players have and their effect on play.
- Identify whether you are playing social or competitive mixed doubles.
- Review the strategies for social doubles.
- Review the strategies for competitive doubles.
- Improve your emotional control, and be sensitive to the emotions of your partner.

Staying Single

In part II, we focused exclusively on doubles play because that is the game of choice for the majority of recreational players, especially as they enter their 50s. But that's not the whole story. Many avid and hardy souls love the enticement of singles play and recognize the inherent benefits in sticking to the one-on-one game. Others like to sprinkle in some singles play with their regular doubles play. It surely won't hurt to understand and develop singles skills to add variety, convenience, and new challenges to your tennis experience.

We assume you have read and absorbed earlier chapters that lay out fundamental strategic principles and advice for tennis skill technique. Based on that assumption, the following chapters will help you understand the similarities between strategy and technique for singles and doubles and their distinct differences. Although both games are played on a tennis court with slightly different dimensions using the same equipment, the strategy, tactics, and technique are significantly different. Many beginning players confuse the two games and end up being dissatisfied with their play because they misunderstand the differences.

Many players who never play singles believe it is simply too physically demanding at their age. A significant difference between singles and doubles is that in singles, you have to serve or return on every point and then play every other shot until the point is concluded. There is no time for rest during play. On the other hand, if you examine the hints for modifying your game after age 50 in the next two chapters, you'll likely be able to compensate for any lack of endurance during a match.

As we did for doubles, let's take a look at some of the distinct advantages of singles play. Perhaps the most obvious is that you'll likely get more physical exercise and experience more exertion from singles because you have more court to cover from side to side. A doubles court is 36 feet (10.9 meters) wide, but each player has only 18 feet (5.5 meters) to defend. In contrast, the singles court is 27 feet (8.3 meters) wide, and you are the lone defender of the additional 9 feet (2.7 meters) plus the angles on both sides. This means more court to cover, more running, and usually a better overall physical workout.

Usually it is easier to arrange singles games because you have to find only one other person rather than three. Schedule adjustments may be simpler as well.

For players who love the challenge of individual competition and pressure, singles offers an opportunity for complete self-reliance. It also prevents you from blaming a poor performance on your partner. Singles play does not require teamwork or sensitivity to a partner. You can focus totally on your own performance.

Singles requires acquiring and improving different technique skills from doubles, and that challenge can be exciting and rewarding. The strategy and tactics for singles play also are clearly different from doubles and the change keeps you mentally sharp by forcing you to adjust to a different game plan.

If you worry about being able to physically endure playing singles, make some simple scoring adjustments. Instead of playing the best of three sets, play two sets and, if necessary, play a 10-point tiebreak instead of a third set to determine the winner. To reduce the number of deuce games that can go on and on, play no-ad scoring. When the score reaches deuce, the player who wins the next point wins the game. The receiver chooses which side of the court to receive the serve on.

Play minisets or shortened sets. We like to play sets where it takes four games to win, but you must win by two. If the score becomes tied at 4-4, play a tiebreak to determine the outcome. This simple adjustment may allow you to play three sets comfortably yet retains the excitement and challenge of a typical match.

Play one pro set in which a player must win 10 games to win the match and be ahead by at least two games. Play for a set amount of time. For example, play for an hour and the player who wins the most games is the winner. This helps limit the length of the match, forces you to focus throughout, and still allows you to do other things that day besides recover from an exhausting match.

As you move into the next chapters on strategy and tennis technique, be sure to note the differences between doubles and singles. If you are able to absorb these distinctions, practice them, and execute them on the court, you may find that you get hooked on singles play just like you did on doubles.

Singles Strategy and Tactics

In the introduction to part III, we discussed the reasons you might prefer singles to doubles and how adding singles play can add variety and challenge your skills and strategies. Now it is time to take a look at the similarities and differences in strategy between the games of singles and doubles.

The most obvious difference in playing singles compared to doubles is that you must cover a greater distance laterally because the singles court (figure 8.1) is 27 feet (8.3 meters) wide and you have no teammate to help cover it. If you add up the number of feet, you have to cover an additional 9 feet (2.7 meters) plus the angles on both sides. This difference changes the physical requirements by demanding more movement and strategic options because the angles and physics of the court are changed both offensively and defensively.

As we did in part II on doubles play, we'll begin with a thorough examination of the strategy and tactics of singles play. You'll remember that we approach things this way to help you better understand why and when it is best to play certain shots before considering how to play them, which will be covered in the next chapter on singles technique.

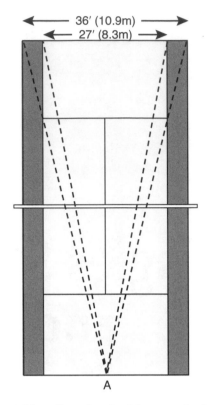

Figure 8.1   Singles court. The alleys for doubles are shaded out.

Strategic Similarities to Doubles

The best strategy in singles tennis is to understand the court dimensions, the relevant laws of physics, and the racket skills that will increase your percentages of winning the majority of points. Just as in doubles play, the singles strategy and tactics are founded on the principles of percentage play, your strengths and weaknesses, and your opponent's strengths and weaknesses.

Percentage play using strategic principles helps you determine an overall plan of attack and defense. A tactical game plan takes into account the strengths and weaknesses of both you and your opponent and helps you adjust your game plan for each match.

Just as in doubles, the crosscourt shot is the foundation of singles play. The reasons are the same, too—the net is lower in the middle and the distance across the court on the diagonal line is longer, thereby offering a safer shot than one directed down the sideline.

Errors rather than winners determine the outcome of a match at every level of play. Some errors are forced by the opponent and some are unforced, but errors always outnumber outright winning shots, often even among professional players. The moral of the story is that you need to be able to keep the ball in play.

Balls hit down the middle of the court reduce the possible angles for your opponent and reduce your risk of hitting wide. A ball hit down the middle that lands deep in your opponent's backcourt offers her few shot options other than returning the ball back down the middle to you.

Aim points for shots are important in singles, too, although their location in the court is different from doubles. The principle of never risking the sideline or baseline still makes good sense. Some players even aim their shots for the deep corners of the court. This is a double gamble since you are risking two lines, both the sideline and the baseline, on one shot. Figure 8.2 shows the optimal aim points that lower your risk of hitting shots wide or deep.

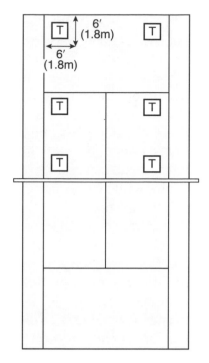

Figure 8.2   Aim points.

Knowing a variety of skills and techniques enables you to play successfully against any type of player, combat the elements, and have success on different court surfaces. You also may confuse and confound your opponent who has to deal with your assortment of offerings if you vary the speed, spin, and angle of your shots. Versatile tactics allow you to make specific adjustments to your overall strategy by adopting a game plan to attack an opponent's weaknesses and avoid his strengths.

Singles positioning is based on the same principle as doubles play. Bisecting the angles of possible returns will put you in the optimal position to play any shot from your opponent. Although the principle of bisecting the angles remains the same from doubles to singles, the difference, of course, is that only one person is available to bisect the angle rather than two.

Controlling your mind and emotions is essential for optimizing your physical performance. The skills of improving focus, managing mistakes, and playing under pressure are identical to those for doubles. And now you've traded worrying about your partner's mental and emotional state to focusing solely on your own with no one to help you.

Strategic Differences From Doubles

Perhaps the most striking difference between singles and doubles play is that the singles tennis court appears quite long and narrow without the addition of the doubles alleys. But looks can be deceiving. As we pointed out, you actually have more area to cover laterally because the width of a singles court—all 27 feet (8.3 meters)—is all yours to defend.

Positioning to bisect the angle of possible returns in singles requires that when you are at the baseline, you actually stay diagonally opposite the ball to protect against a wide-angle return. It is extremely rare for all four players in doubles to be at the baseline at the same time, so this method of bisecting the angles is rarely needed in doubles. However, in singles, much of the play is from the baseline. You have to learn to play the possible angles while exchanging baseline rallies with your opponent.

Because no players start a point at the net, the journey to gain the net is more difficult and happens less frequently. Points end most often before either player gets to the net position. Therefore consistency and depth in baseline shots become important in forcing your opponent into a defensive position because you have no partner at the net to pose a threat. Because your opponent will never begin a point at the net, hit ground strokes higher over the net (about 3 to 5 feet [1 to 1.5 meters]), which will add depth to your shots and pin your opponent behind the baseline.

The percentage play for placement of the first serve may be to the outside of the service box to force your opponent wide to one side off the court, thereby opening up the whole court for your next shot. Moving your opponent side to side and up and back becomes the foundation of your strategy because she has more court to cover and no one else to rely on.

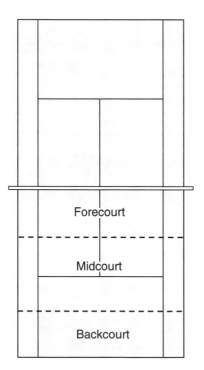

Figure 8.3 **Areas of the court: backcourt, midcourt, and forecourt.**

Strategies for the Backcourt

When you are in the backcourt (figure 8.3) near the baseline, have a mind-set of neutrality so you don't attempt a risky offensive shot. Concentrate on playing consistently and error free. The best formula from the backcourt is to hit crosscourt to take advantage of the lower net in the middle and longer court length and to aim the ball higher over the net to gain depth and reduce the chance of an error.

When receiving serve, the fundamental return should be crosscourt or down the middle of the court to neutralize the serve. As the rally begins, aim for depth and the aim points shown in figure 8.2 (page 117). Chances are good that one player or the other will make an error during the rally and lose the point. However, if the point continues and your opponent hits a short ball into the midcourt, approach by hitting a ball down the line and moving to the net.

During the rally, quickly return to your home base after each shot. Notice in figure 8.4, *a* and *b,* that home base is *not* the center of the court but rather the center of your opponent's possible angles. Your rule of thumb is to stay diagonally opposite the ball when both of you are at the baseline.

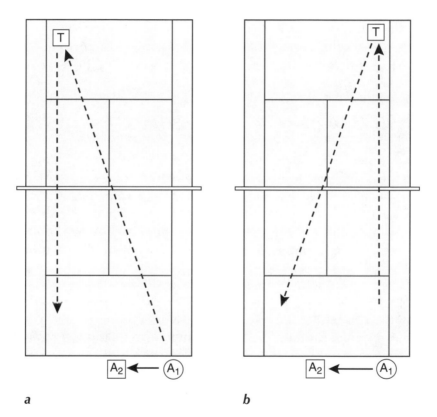

a   *b*

Figure 8.4   **Bisecting the angle:** *(a)* **crosscourt shot;** *(b)* **down-the-line shot.**

☻ Practice Tip: Figure-8 Drill

An excellent way to reinforce the value of crosscourt shots is to spar with a partner from the baseline. Hit the ball at three-fourths speed. One player hits every shot crosscourt, and the other player hits down the line. This is often called the figure-8 drill. You'll quickly see that the player who hits down the line will do much more running. You'll have to switch roles frequently.

Strategies for the Midcourt

When you are in the midcourt, put pressure on your opponent but use caution. Although winners are possible from this position, it is wise to try them only if you can contact the ball above the height of the net from a balanced position. The best formula for the midcourt is to hit the ball straight along the sideline and follow the ball to the net position in the forecourt and make sure the flight of the ball leaving your racket is straight ahead, neither up nor down.

When you get a short ball that lands in the midcourt, the percentage play is a down-the-line approach shot. However, after you've worked that pattern a few times, you may find your opponent scrambling to cover that shot as soon as she hits a short ball. In that case, you may decide to hit crosscourt behind her to take advantage of the element of surprise. Another possible option is to gently hit a drop shot crosscourt to confuse her.

HITTING AN EFFECTIVE APPROACH SHOT

The key to an effective approach shot is to aim for depth by flattening your swing so the ball moves through the court and does not set up your opponent. Whether you apply backspin or topspin depends on your arsenal of shots, but some spin is necessary to control the depth. Because you are closer to the net than you would be for a normal ground stroke, your backswing should be only half to three-fourths its normal length to keep your approach shot from hitting the fence.

Normally, you hit the approach shot down the line to allow yourself to move into the forecourt and bisect the angle of possible returns with just two or three steps. If you approach crosscourt, you'll put yourself in the position of having to cross the centerline and move at least four or five steps to bisect the possible returns. Look at figure 8.5, *a* and *b,* to see the differences.

Strategies for the Forecourt

When you reach the forecourt at the net, aim to win the point outright with a well-placed volley or an overhead smash. Your chance of hitting a winner depends on the difficulty of the oncoming ball in terms of speed, spin, and height; your opponent's position on the court; and how close to

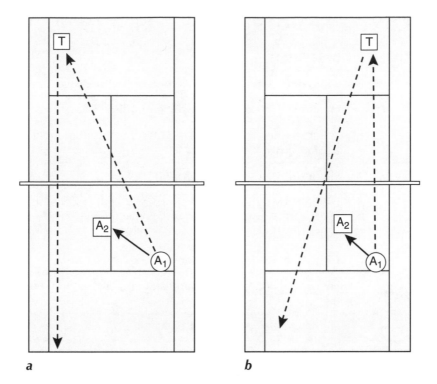

Figure 8.5 **Bisecting the angle after an approach shot:** *(a)* **crosscourt approach;** *(b)* **down-the-line approach.**

the net you are able to get. It may take a two-shot combination to conclude the point, so patience may be required.

The best formula from the forecourt is to aim the ball crosscourt to the open court but cover the possible angle of returns in case your opponent reaches the shot and to make sure the ball moves downward as it leaves your racket if you can hit the ball above the net. If your opponent hits a low passing shot, you will probably be better off playing a low volley deep down the line and waiting for the next shot.

Some players find it helpful to think of the three areas of the court in the context of traffic lights. In the backcourt, the light is red, and you are simply sparring for position with your opponent. In the midcourt, the light is yellow, and you should proceed with caution with a forcing approach shot or occasionally try for a winner only if you are perfectly balanced and playing a ball that is above the height of the net. In the forecourt, the light is clearly green, and you should end the point with a volley or overhead placement provided you can contact the ball above the height of the net. The chart "High-Percentage Shots in Singles" summarizes the high-percentage shots from each area of the court and for specific game situations.

HIGH PERCENTAGE SHOTS IN SINGLES

GAME SITUATION	BEST SHOT
Serving	Hit to outside third of service box or returner's weakness.
Receiving	Hit crosscourt deep or down the middle.
During rally	Hit crosscourt deep, down the middle, or to opponent's weaker stroke.
At baseline	Hit upward on serve and ground strokes.
At midcourt	Hit ball down the line and approach net, hit winner to open court, or hit drop shot to surprise opponent; hit ball straight with no arc.
At net	Hit to open court; hit ball downward.
Lobbing	Hit over opponent's backhand side; hit crosscourt when possible.
Hitting overhead smash	Hit crosscourt on diagonal.

Key Singles Game Strategies

Once you understand and integrate the concepts of strategy from each distinct area of the court, you can begin to implement a half dozen other strategies that have been proved over time to be sound. Let's take a look at each in turn.

Hit to Opponent's Weakness

This may seem obvious, but it is not always easy to implement. The backhand is the weakest shot for many players, and balls that bounce high to the backhand are especially difficult to handle. If your opponent's backhand is weak, hit most balls to that side of the court and force your opponent into errors or weak shots. You might also want to approach the net by hitting to that side even if it means playing the ball crosscourt from the midcourt, which is usually not a smart play.

Most players who have a weak backhand try to cover it up by hitting more forehands. If that is the case with your opponent, you may have to hit a shot or two to his forehand to force him to one side of the court before hitting to his backhand.

One other caution about picking a weaker shot. Many players hit the backhand defensively but rarely miss. Although their forehand may appear to be the stronger shot, it also might elicit the most errors because they try to hit a more forcing shot on the forehand side. Test each side carefully, and tactically adjust your game to your opponent's weakness.

Another overlooked weakness is that many steady baseline players are comfortable from the backcourt but uncertain at the net. Although it seems counterintuitive to draw your opponent forward into the attacking position, if her volleys and overheads are somewhat erratic, this can be an excellent tactic.

Hit to the Open Court

Another fundamental strategy is to hit to the open court. This will force your opponent to run to the ball and rush the shot or hit a weak return. This strategy takes advantage of the relatively wider singles court. Test your opponent's physical condition by moving him side to side.

The danger with this strategy is that if your opponent returns your crosscourt shot with his own crosscourt shot, you will be tempted to hit down the sideline to make him run. That puts you in the position of changing the direction of the ball, which is somewhat more difficult to do, and risking the higher net at the sideline. Therefore, stick to the crosscourt shot until you elicit a weak response and then attack from the midcourt.

Practice Tip: Opening up the Court

A great way to practice hitting to the open court is to begin a point with a wide serve to the outside of the service box (figure 8.6). The receiver must hit the return down the line or to the middle. The server then hits the next shot crosscourt to the open court. The point ends after the three shots, and the score is recorded if either player makes an error. The crosscourt shot must land in the deep quadrant of the court to earn a point for the server.

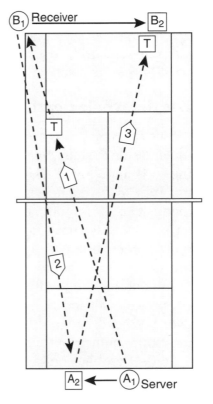

Figure 8.6 **Opening up the court with the serve.**

Hit Behind Your Opponent

The next logical strategy to use after hitting to the open court several times is to surprise your opponent by hitting back to the spot from which she played the last shot. Chances are if you've been hitting to the open court, she'll begin to anticipate that shot and hustle over to cover the open side. When she begins to do that, simply direct the ball back to the spot she came from. She may try to change direction, but in most cases it will be a futile move. This strategy is particularly effective against a very quick opponent who anticipates well and seems to cover the court well. She'll become the victim of her own speed if you keep her honest.

Practice Tip: Hitting Behind the Opponent

Use the same setup as the drill on hitting to the open court. Only this time, after the serve and the return down the line or to the middle, direct the third shot to where the receiver came from (figure 8.7). To make it realistic, the receiver must move at least to the center hash mark as if he were sprinting to cover the open court. The server then must place the ball in the deep quadrant of the court to win the point.

Use the Whole Court

Most singles players get quite comfortable moving side to side while hitting alternating forehands and backhands. Although this may involve a fair amount of movement, it pales in comparison to forcing an opponent to move up to the net and back to recover a lob. If you really want to test the fitness and endurance of your opponent, hit short balls to entice her to come to the net and then lob the next ball over her head and force her to retreat. A few trips up and back will tire most opponents.

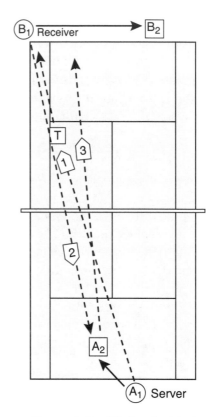

Figure 8.7 Hitting behind the opponent.

To deliver the coup de grace, direct your first shot deep to one side followed by a short one to the other side of the court. Then lob your third shot back in the direction of your first shot to make your opponent not only move up and back but also cover both sides of the court.

These are terrific strategies, but they take skill to execute. Practice them with a willing partner so that you can control the depth and direction of your shots. Once you've mastered these shot sequences, you will have a terrific pattern of play that will test any opponent. See figure 8.8 to see the typical pattern of up-and-back and side-to-side shots.

Open the Court With Angles

Most players assume they have to cover the court only from sideline to sideline. The truth is, if you give your opponent a sharply angled shot, he may reply with a sharply angled shot of his own that draws you well beyond the sideline to retrieve it (figure 8.9). You may end up hitting balls from a position 6 or 8 feet (1.8 or 2.4 meters) wide of the sideline. So why not turn that strategy around and use it on your opponent? Let him cover the 27 feet (8.3 meters) of court area plus another 6 to 8 feet (1.8 or 2.4 meters) on each side.

The time to hit a sharply angled shot is when you receive a ball that lands wide to the side of your court. A ball hit near the center is difficult to direct

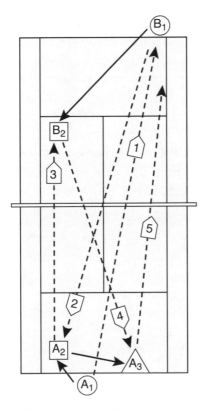

Figure 8.8 Move your opponent side to side and up and back.

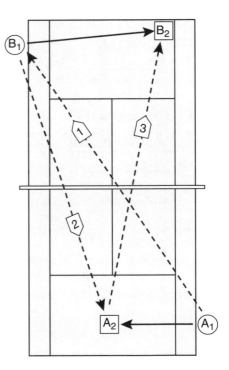

Figure 8.9 Use a wide shot to open up the court.

wide, so don't risk a wide shot unless you first receive a wide ball. If you've drawn your opponent wide outside the sideline and she replies with a shot down the line or to the middle, direct your next shot crosscourt to the open court. Chances are you'll be able to celebrate a winning shot.

By this time you've probably guessed that if you are pulled wide, the best shot is crosscourt with enough height to give yourself time to recover back into the court. Occasionally a shot down the line will catch your opponent napping, but the risk of the shot over the high part of the net and shorter court distance is usually a poor idea, and if your opponent does reach the shot and plays it crosscourt, you'll be lucky to reach it.

Use Favorite Patterns of Play

Patterns of play are simply a sequence of shots that exploit your opponent's weaknesses or enhance your court position. If you watch experienced players or professionals, you can see that their game is composed of patterns that are repeated.

Patterns begin with the serve and return and build in variety as the point develops. Each of the patterns you use should be sound strategically and designed to give you an advantage over an opponent. Of course, opponents vary widely in their own skills and fitness levels, so you will need several trusty patterns you can use, depending on your opponent. And don't forget that if you play a left-handed player, you have to reverse your patterns.

To master a sequence of shots, simply practice that sequence over and over. Match play is a poor time to try a new pattern; instead, practice with a buddy and agree to work on patterns you believe will be effective for you. As you test them against different opponents, you'll find that some patterns work against most players and some have only limited use. File away those observations and retrieve them each time you meet a new opponent.

Styles of Play

You have learned that overall strategy is a combination of sound percentage tennis, your strengths and weaknesses, and your opponent's strengths and weaknesses. Earlier in this chapter you learned the principles of percentage tennis, the geometry of the tennis court, and the preferred shot for most situations during play. At this point you may want to fine-tune your

---

For a more detailed discussion of more than 50 patterns of play complete with diagrams, check out the book *Tennis Tactics: Winning Patterns of Play* by the United States Tennis Association, Human Kinetics, 1996.

game by adopting a style of play that fits your skills, physical abilities, and mental characteristics. Based on their general style of play in singles, players usually can be grouped into these categories: all-court players, aggressive baseliners, serve-and-volleyers, and counterpunchers.

As players move into the 50-and-older age category, style of play tends to become a blend of styles because of diminishing ability to hit with pace, especially on the serve; limited court movement; and less emphasis on the serve-and-volley style, even for those who used that style in the past.

Tennis after 50 tends to rely more on shotmaking ability because players have likely added a variety of shots over years of play and can focus more on accuracy, variety, change of speed, and spins than in earlier years. Chances are players are also more patient because points tend to last longer, and fewer winners are struck.

All-court players are typically athletic, cover the court well, use a wide variety of shots, and are able to adjust the speed, spin, and placement of their shots. They can shift back and forth from offense to defense as dictated by their opponents or the match situation. Usually, all-court players have no glaring weaknesses but also may not have any outstanding weapons. Mentally, all-court players are clever in exposing an opponent's weaknesses and do not hesitate to exploit a weakness relentlessly.

Aggressive baseliners appear frequently on the professional tour. They have developed deep, penetrating ground strokes that keep their opponents on the defense and possess at least one outstanding weapon (forehand or backhand), which they use to hit outright winners from the midcourt or even the backcourt. The pace, depth, and power behind their ground strokes make them formidable opponents during a rally. Precise footwork, balance, and the ability to hit the ball as it rises are also distinguishing characteristics. Aggressive baseliners enjoy taking calculated risks and tend to dominate nearly every point.

Serve-and-volleyers seem to be lacking on the professional tour, but there are always a few young players who show promise of developing this style. Most of the great serve-and-volley players of the past have had excellent serves, sound volleys, unusual reach and quick reactions at the net, and a devastating overhead smash. Typically, they are tall, have an aggressive personality, and enjoy playing a high-risk game.

Counterpunchers tend to be excellent at covering the court; to be in great physical condition; and to possess steady ground strokes, consistent lobs, and excellent passing shots. Their plan is to retrieve every ball and force their opponents into errors through long, tiring points. They are patient and exult if they can tease their opponents into a low-percentage shot and eventual error.

You may recognize your style of play among these classic four descriptions. Or perhaps your style is undefined and could use development. Keep in mind the physical and mental characteristics required for each style and move toward the one that most closely follows your natural temperament and physical skills.

Your personal style of play may vary depending on your opponent. At times, you'll probably have to adjust your style to deal with a particular player, the court surface, or weather conditions. Try playing different styles against players who are a bit below your normal level and see if you can adapt to more than one rigid style of play.

On very windy days you may need to adjust your ground strokes by using a shorter backswing and getting into a balanced position before the shot so you can make a last-second adjustment if the wind suddenly alters the flight of the ball. If you play on a slower court surface such as a damp, clay court after a shower, patience is required because you and your opponent will return more shots and it will be difficult for both of you to end the point. Playing against a counterpunching player who lobs a lot will be especially frustrating on a damp clay court. You may have a tendency to overhit your shots in hopes of ending the point and suffer the ignominy of making a steady stream of errors instead.

In addition to determining your own style of play, you'll also have to learn how to play against opponents who use each of the styles and learn how to compete against left-handed players. This is where the tactical fun becomes the key to success. Ending a point against a persistent counterpuncher or breaking the serve of a serve-and-volley player are unique skills that take planning and serious practice or match experience.

Practice Tip: Role Playing

Assign yourself a style of play that is different from normal and play an entire set using that style. You'll improve your skills doing this. If you can convince a partner to play a particular style, you can also work on your tactics to counter each of the styles. Try handicapping methods to make play more realistic. For example, allow the counterpuncher only one serve and agree that he cannot come to the net.

Adjusting Singles Strategy After Age 50

If you've kept yourself in great physical condition and have been blessed by a lack of major injuries, you may be able to play pretty much the same style you've always played for another 10 years or so. Eventually, though, loss of physical strength, stamina, and flexibility will creep up on you, too. It's far better to have alternative strategies for compensating in mind before your game deteriorates too quickly for you to recover and still enjoy playing.

Also you need to recognize the limitations of your opponents who are over 50 and reevaluate your tactical plan when you play them. And if you are playing younger players, design strategies to frustrate them and neutralize their typical physical advantages by outsmarting them. Try the following strategies depending on your style of game, the opponents you play, and your personal health and vigor.

Minimize Effort Expended

When you watch experienced and successful older players, try to determine the amount of effort they expend on every point. Typically, there is no wasted motion before or during a point. Movements are efficient and precise and appear smooth, unhurried, and relaxed. Inside, the mental process is in high gear: They compute angles and make decisions quickly and automatically.

Good balance is evident on every shot because an experienced player uses small steps to adjust to the oncoming ball rather than lunging awkwardly. When the ball is on the other side of the net, the savvy player is moving into the best defensive position.

You'll also see that smart players emphasize getting their first serves in, thereby conserving energy. They rarely make unforced errors, especially on returns of serve. You can achieve consistency when serving and receiving by allowing yourself a greater margin of error, aiming well inside the lines, and never hitting the ball into the net.

Shrink the Court

After age 50, your willingness and ability to move forward to the net and back to retrieve a lob are likely to abate to some degree. One way to reduce the occurrence of repeated up-and-back movement is to shrink the length of the court by playing inside the baseline at three-fourths of the court or even at the service line. This position forces your opponent to try to hit at your feet and gives you an opportunity to play the ball out of the air rather than retreating to play a normal ground stroke. If you move into the service line area, you'll take away your opponent's ability to lob over your head.

If you decide this is a worthwhile tactic, practice hitting low volleys and half-volleys because your opponent is certain to aim for your feet. (See chapter 9 for specific hints on the technique for low volleys and half-volleys.) Once you feel comfortable playing low shots, you'll probably force your opponent to press for an even better shot, which may force an error. Because you are taking the ball earlier than you would from the baseline, your opponent will have less time to react to your shot. An added bonus is that as you move closer to the net, more angles will be available to you to open the court and move your opponent laterally.

Anticipate Every Shot

Veteran players seem to run less during points because they anticipate the opponent's shot. We'll explain how you can do it too.

Know the best shot in each situation during a point and defend against that shot, forcing your opponent to increase her risk by trying for more pace or trying a more reckless shot. (See the chart "High-Percentage Shots in Singles" on page 122 for a list of the high-percentage shots.) Keep a running mental record of the shots your opponent played in each situation during the match. As the match develops, run to the spot to defend the shot she has favored and force her into an alternative. Watch carefully as your opponent prepares to strike the ball for giveaway signs as to which shot she will hit. Many players will tip you off by opening the racket face too soon, changing their stance, or turning their body prematurely.

In every case, if your opponent has gained the edge during the rally and is preparing to end the point, anticipate that shot and move early to intercept it. You can't simply wait until she plays the shot and react because you'll be too late. If you guess wrong, nothing has been lost because you would not have reached the ball anyway.

Vary the Pace, Spin, and Height

In baseball and softball, successful pitchers who have long careers have refined their skills as they age and learned to rely less on throwing fast pitches past the batter. Veteran pitchers change speeds, spins, and locations, forcing the batter to adjust to every pitch and making it difficult for the batter to anticipate the next pitch.

Likewise, in tennis, frustrate your opponent by constantly changing the speed, spin, placement, and height of the ball during a rally. Vary your serving, too, by mixing in different spins and speeds to disrupt your opponent's timing. This strategy of using a variety of shots will prevent your opponent from feeling grooved in his shots and probably will frustrate him. Keep him even more frustrated by reducing your errors and forcing him to play multiple shots just to stay in the point.

Use Short Shots, Drop Shots, and Lobs

By now you probably realize that moving up to the net and back is the most physically taxing move in tennis. Test an opponent's endurance by intentionally hitting short balls or drop shots that force her to expend a lot of effort just to reach the ball. Chances are she'll hit a weak reply and you'll be able to pass her at the net fairly easily. If she manages to hit an offensive or neutralizing shot, simply lob over her head and let her decide whether it is worth running down your lob or giving up the point.

One critical tip for using short shots to bring your opponent in—don't risk trying to hit short if you are at your baseline or behind it. An intentionally short shot takes too long to cross the net and may allow your opponent to reach it easily. Rather, if you can play a shot from the three-fourths court or closer, a short shot or drop shot can be deadly in your favor.

Playing Against a Younger Opponent

After age 50, you shouldn't limit yourself to playing other players over 50. In fact, you'll widen your choice of potential opponents by playing people of all ages. If you choose to play a younger opponent, use these tips for coping with a stronger, faster opponent.

First of all, do not try to match her game. Many younger players hit the ball harder than you do and thus are more prone to errors. Play more conservative shots by hitting deep to the middle of the court, hoping to elicit a short ball. When you get a short ball, you know what to do based on the advice in this chapter.

A second strategy is to vary the height, pace, and spin against a younger opponent. Chances are he'll be frustrated by the variety and try to overhit your clever offerings. You'll put his strong, firm ground strokes and timing to a severe test if he tries to generate a lot of power from your slower-paced shots.

Third, move your opponent up and back with drop shots, dinks, and angled shots and then lob to chase her back to the baseline. Chances are her pride in her powerful ground strokes will crumble as she is forced to play unfamiliar shots repeatedly.

WORDS TO THE WISE

- Understand the similarities and differences between doubles strategy and singles strategy. Recognize that you and your opponent have more court to cover and play accordingly.

- Understand the best-percentage shot from the backcourt, midcourt, and forecourt. Stick with the percentages most of the time except if your opponent has obvious strengths or weaknesses that take precedence.

- Note the aim points in figure 8.2 (page 117) and use them as targets for every shot. There is little reason to risk aiming close to the line unless you are feeling very lucky that day.

- Practice the key strategies in singles and build consistent patterns of play that work for you against most opponents. Those patterns should become the essence of your personal style of play.

- Develop your own style of play and determine the style of your opponent early in the match. Once those styles are clear, match your game plan to the challenge you face.

- Adjust your game as you age and learn to rely more on variety, tactics, anticipation, and use of the whole court. You'll find the game of singles to be even more challenging and intellectually stimulating than ever before.

Technique Skills for Singles

The previous chapter detailed the key strategic and tactical principles of playing singles in tennis. Now we need to take a look at tennis technique to help you accomplish those strategies through efficient, effective racket work and the supporting body positioning.

As a start, we suggest that you review chapter 6 on doubles technique, paying particular attention to the information at the beginning of the chapter through the heading Forced or Unforced Errors. This advice applies to both singles and doubles. Rather than repeat racket technique here that is the same for both games, we'll simply point out the commonalities and then discuss the differences in technique between singles and doubles skills.

Technique Similarities

There are more similarities in stroke technique between singles and doubles than there are differences. That's why so many players move easily from one game to the other during their tennis careers and enjoy the variety of playing both games.

In chapter 6, we introduced the importance of learning to rally effectively as the foundation of the game. In singles play, the rally takes on added significance because more points are played from the baseline than at the net.

The technique for racket work on strokes is identical for singles and doubles as is the advice for controlling shots by altering height, depth, spin, speed, and direction. Body balance and dynamic movement around the court follow the same model in both games, ensuring efficiency of movement and support for stroke technique.

Rally Foundation

In chapter 2 we introduced the idea of learning to rally as the first step in playing tennis, and that holds true for both singles and doubles. Rallying with a friend can be a great physical workout, and learning to keep the ball in play during a rally is the first requirement for playing the game.

Many players, especially beginners, try to hit the ball too hard at first and thus end up making frequent errors. Scale back the power of your shots to about 75 percent of your maximum and aim to land 5 to 10 shots in succession over the net and into the backcourt without an error. If you can consistently play 5 to 10 shots without an error, then you've developed your personal *rally shot*, the shot you can use to begin most points and spar with your opponent in the hopes that she will make an error or hit a weak reply that you can attack.

For new players or players returning after a long layoff, rallying practice is the key skill to focus on. All tennis players are looking for practice partners who can keep the ball in play consistently so they can have fun, get exercise, and groove their strokes. Read the following sections carefully to review the keys to successful play from the baseline and tips to ensure the consistency of your shots.

To promote consistency during a rally, contact the ball about waist high on every shot. To achieve this goal, you'll have to track the flight of the ball and move into position by anticipating the bounce of the ball as it crosses the net. At the crucial moment of impact with the ball, your racket face will determine the direction and height of the shot you deliver over the net. To hit the ball higher, simply open the racket face at contact or close it slightly if your shots are going higher than you intended. Alter the direction of the ball by angling the racket face at the contact point so that your strings point in the direction of your intended shot. To enhance the shot, follow through in that direction through the hitting area.

Overall Tennis Technique

Whether you are playing singles or doubles, the key points of tennis technique as shown in figure 6.1 (page 79) are identical. Even though you may have a bit more time to prepare for a shot in singles because the majority of shots will be played from the backcourt, we still advocate beginning the swing with a unit turn of the racket and shoulders rather than thinking of taking your racket back. By turning your shoulders during the preparation phase, you will set up the proper trunk rotation to generate maximum efficiency and power and will add an element of disguise. Once you execute the shoulder turn, adjust your swing to the oncoming ball and apply the appropriate spin to control the distance of the shot.

🎾 Practice Tip

An excellent test of your readiness to play the ball is to determine whether you have completed the unit turn as the ball crosses or hits the net. If not, you will be too late executing your swing. An alternative is to say to yourself "bounce" as the ball bounces on your side of the net and then "hit" as you contact the ball. Those two cues will help you anticipate the rhythm of the rally.

A corollary to this advice is to adjust the length of your swing to your court position and the speed of the oncoming ball. The closer you are to the net, the shorter the backswing. On the zero-to-five scale we suggested in chapter 6, net shots are best hit with a zero swing, and midcourt shots with a three. In contrast, if you are driving a ball from behind the baseline, a full swing, what we would label a five, is necessary to impart the speed and depth to your shot unless you simply loft it with a moon ball or lob.

Ball Control

The five elements of ball control in singles are identical to the controls in doubles: height, direction, speed, depth or distance, and spin. You will need a clear understanding and fair degree of skill to execute each of these controls because typically the rallies will be longer and more shots will be played from the backcourt in singles than in doubles. You may want to refer to the section on controlling the ball in chapter 6 to refresh your understanding of how to adjust your racket and swing to correct errors.

STROKE DOCTOR

If inconsistency plagues you, and your shots are unpredictable, you are likely lacking control of the racket face throughout the swing. From the beginning of the forward swing and through ball contact, your racket face must be *steady and undisturbed*. Focus on squeezing your grip, which helps keep the racket face moving in the intended direction of your shot.

Body Control and Dynamic Balance

The fundamental principles of body control and dynamic balance are identical to those presented for doubles with a few enhancements.

Maintaining upper-body balance, using the correct footwork, using a split-step or check-step, maintaining optimal muscle tension, and keeping the head still throughout the swing are critical features of stroking the ball. Again, you may want to refresh your memory by rereading the information on body control and balance in chapter 6.

Because you have a larger court area to cover, singles play will more rigorously test your movement skills and dynamic balance, so pay particular attention to those skills. If you need to travel a long distance to get to the ball, take long steps to cover the distance, and as you approach the ball, shorten your steps to adjust your final position for the stroke. Pumping your arms while sprinting longer distances is helpful, but as you near the ball and shorten your final positioning steps, begin your unit turn of the shoulders so you can play the ball without feeling rushed.

Technique Differences for Singles Play

Perhaps the greatest single difference between singles and doubles is the importance of the rally and the frequency of hitting forehands and backhands from the baseline. When we think of playing singles, we think of two players sparring with a rally from the baseline until someone makes an error or one player attacks a short ball and approaches the net. Points tend to last longer in singles because it is more difficult to force an error. As a result, it is essential to develop consistency and patience. In fact, you need to be able to hit several baseline ground strokes in succession just to stay neutral in a singles point. Compare this to doubles, in which you are always looking to gain the net position or set up your partner who is already at the net.

In chapter 8 on singles strategy, you learned that the foundation of singles play is the crosscourt shot that lands deep in your opponent's court. You also learned that the flight of the ball from the baseline must be upward to avoid falling into the net or short in the court. As a result, you must apply spin to the ball to control the distance if you hit the ball with pace.

Stroking Versus Hitting the Ball

It is possible in doubles to be an effective player without being able to stroke the ball, but this is almost impossible in singles play. An inability to stroke the ball repeatedly in singles will almost certainly lead to a string of errors and loss of points.

Think of your ground strokes as a way to apply spin to the ball by stroking, brushing, wiping, or caressing the ball by moving your racket up, down, or across the ball as if you were stroking the fur of a pet. Hitting a ball should be reserved for baseball or softball where the object is to hit for distance. In tennis, controlling the distance so the ball lands in the court is the object of the game.

Using Topspin or Backspin From the Baseline

To have a full repertoire of shots, you should be able to apply topspin or backspin to your ground strokes and vary the amount of spin depending on your tactical objective. And you should know when to use each spin and the relative advantages and disadvantages of one shot over the other.

The optimal drive is hit with topspin so that the ball rotates forward and falls inside the baseline. Once it bounces, the ball tends to continue to move through the court. If you apply heavy spin, your opponent may find it difficult to play the shot. A backspin drive provides an effective change of pace, is easier to time consistently, and, if hit properly, tends to stay low to the court and skid. Strive to be able to apply either topspin or backspin on both forehands and backhands.

Applying topspin to the ball is easier if your grip is well behind the racket on both forehand and backhand. Those grips include a traditional eastern, semiwestern, or western grip (figure 9.1, *a-c*). On the backhand side, the preferred grip is a full eastern backhand or a two-handed grip (figure 9.2, *a* and *b*). Use the continental grip (figure 9.3) for serves and volleys.

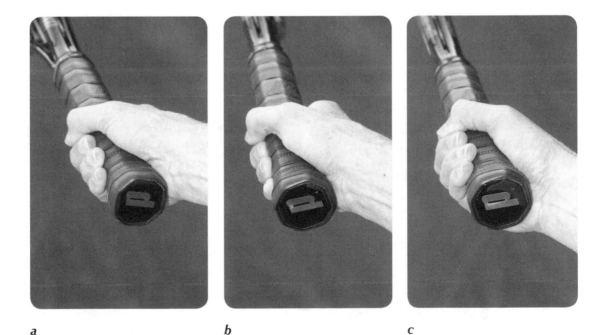

a   *b*   *c*

Figure 9.1   Forehand grips: *(a)* eastern; *(b)* semiwestern; *(c)* western.

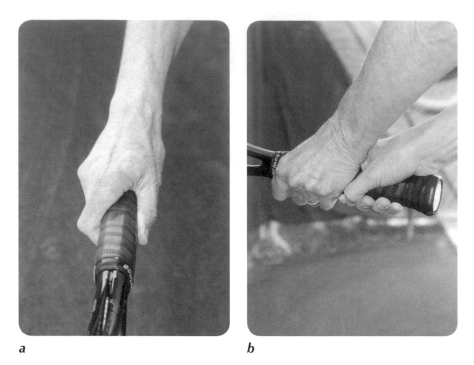

a   b

Figure 9.2   Backhand grips: *(a)* full eastern; *(b)* two handed.

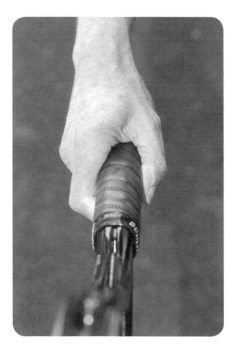

Figure 9.3   Continental grip.

The technique for applying topspin to an oncoming ball is to brush up the back of the ball by moving your racket low to high during the forward swing. The sharper the angle of the upward motion, the more spin you will generate. Heavy topspin is helpful when hitting higher over the net to bring the ball down into the court or when hitting passing shots that you want to land at your opponent's feet.

☌ STROKE DOCTOR

To increase the amount of topspin on the ball, lower your body and racket head below the ball and lift up as you swing forward. Accelerate the racket and finish with the racket over your opposite shoulder pointing toward the back fence (figure 9.4). To get the feel of brushing up the back of the ball, use a multicolored beach ball so that you can see it spin forward. Place your open hand below the center of the ball and push your arm forward and up at a 45-degree angle to make the ball rotate forward.

To decrease the amount of topspin and gain more depth on ground strokes, move your racket toward the intended target during the forward swing and decrease the angle of upward movement. Finish the shot in the direction of the ball's flight (figure 9.5).

Figure 9.4 When applying heavy topspin, finish with the racket over the opposite shoulder.

Figure 9.5 To gain depth and reduce spin on the shot, finish with the racket head in the direction of the shot.

Applying backspin to the ball requires a slightly open racket face during the forward swing. Lead the swing with the bottom edge of the racket. The beauty of backspin is that it is somewhat safer than topspin because the amount of time the racket stays in contact with the ball during the hitting phase is longer and the contact is easier to time. However, once the ball

Figure 9.6 Thrust the opposite arm back while moving the racket arm forward on a slice backhand.

is in flight and bounces, the fact that the ball is spinning in the opposite direction of the flight reduces the speed and penetration of the shot into the court.

If your backspin shots seem to lack force and appear to float a bit because there is too much spin, you are probably swinging too steeply in a high-to-low path and in the process applying too much spin. Adjust your technique by swinging on a more level plane and allowing the slightly open racket face to apply the spin. The result will be a drive that is flatter with some backspin to help control the depth of the shot.

Add power to your backspin backhand by thrusting your free arm back toward the fence at the same time you move your racket arm forward toward the net (figure 9.6). The opposing forces keep your shoulders sideways to the net and the racket moving through the path of the intended ball flight.

STROKE DOCTOR

If your backhand is weak, check your grip first to be sure your hand is behind the racket. Next, be certain your arm is close to your body during the backswing and point the back of your front shoulder at the oncoming ball. This position ensures that you will use the larger muscles of your upper body to generate racket head speed instead of simply using your arm. Finally, check the position where you contact the ball. For a backspin shot, the contact point should be even with the front foot and for a topspin drive, about 6 inches (15 centimeters) in front of the front foot. A late contact point will produce a weak shot.

Many players who use a shake-hands, or continental, grip find it easier to apply backspin than topspin to the ball because the racket face is naturally slightly open as they meet the ball. Another advantage of this grip is that you do not have to change grips to play a forehand, backhand, serve, or volley. The trade-off however is a somewhat weaker grip; more difficulty in imparting topspin; and high, bouncing shots.

Hitting for Depth

During a rally, the most grievous mistake you can make is to hit a shot into the net. This is a silly error because on most shots hit from the baseline to an opponent at his baseline, you should aim to clear the net by 3 to 5 feet (1 to 1.5 meters). Thus, a ball that lands in the net means you missed your target by a considerable margin. Eliminating balls into the net will add at least a few points in your favor every match you play.

Another reason you should clear the net by a good margin is that it will send the ball deeper into your opponent's court and prevent him from attacking. Of course, you can accomplish this objective by hitting every ball harder, but the risk is much greater. If you change the pace of the ball during a point, you will complicate things for your opponent.

STROKE DOCTOR

If your shots consistently land short on medium-paced shots, try reducing the amount of spin you apply. Less spin means the ball will travel a greater distance, thus landing deep in the court on the other side of the net. At the same time you are reducing the spin on the ball, aim higher over the net. Your shot's higher trajectory will help guide it deeper into your opponent's court. Greater depth comes from a combination of less spin and more height on your shots.

Footwork and Stance

The footwork you use to cover the singles court and your stance to strike the ball are more challenging in singles. This is because you have more court to cover, and you need to drive the ball more often from behind your baseline deep into your opponent's court.

A closed stance in which your front foot is closer to the sideline you are facing than the rear foot is, is the most ineffective and inefficient stance for playing the ball. By stepping across your body line, you lock your hips, particularly on the forehand drive, thereby decreasing the power you get from rotating your hips. An added disadvantage is that your body weight moves sideways rather than in the direction of the intended flight of the ball.

In a more traditional square stance, you line up sideways to the oncoming ball so that the toes of both feet are parallel. Just before striking the ball, shift your body weight forward and into the shot to produce a solid shot.

In the past 20 years, more and more players have begun hitting ground strokes from an open stance (figure 9.7a). In this case, the rear foot is closer to the sideline you are facing. If you begin the stroke with a full unit turn

Figure 9.7 Stances: *(a)* open; *(b)* closed; *(c)* square.

of the shoulders, the energy that is stored from the stretch of your muscles is available to transfer into the shot as you rotate your body during the forward swing. You apply power in succession as your legs push against the ground, your hips rotate, and then your upper body rotates. This action produces more power with less effort than either the closed (figure 9.7*b*) or square stance (figure 9.7*c*).

As an added bonus, if you use open footwork on both forehand and backhand, you'll be able to plant the outside foot toward the sideline and push off it to recover for the next shot. This move is more economical and simpler than a crossing step, improving your ability to cover the court easily. Watch the professional players from the baseline and notice the frequent use of open footwork.

Serving and Receiving

The serving technique in singles should be similar to that of doubles, but you may want to take more risk with placement and speed. Strategically, a strong serve to the outside third of the court opens the court for your next shot. You may find that easier to achieve by adding slice with sidespin so that the ball actually curves in flight. For right-handers, the wide slice serve is effective in the deuce court. For lefties, it is best used in the ad court.

APPLYING SIDESPIN TO THE SERVE

To apply sidespin to the serve, a right-handed player should imagine aiming at a clock face. For a flat serve, contact the ball between 12:00 and 1:00. To add sidespin, contact the ball at about 2:00. The racket face meets the ball on a slight angle.

At the fundamental level, think of serving as an overhand throwing motion similar to that used by a quarterback in football or a baseball player. In fact, an excellent first step in learning to serve is to practice the throwing motion from the baseline over the net and into the court. Just like on ground strokes, the flight of the ball when it leaves your racket on the serve must be *upward*. Despite what many people think, the laws of gravity prevent you from serving down into the service box unless you are taller than 6 feet, 5 inches (1.9 meters). The upward motion allows your serve to clear the net. Impart topspin to the ball to bring it down into the court.

Speed on the serve comes from a push with your legs from the ground and an uncoiling of your body from the hips, trunk, shoulder, elbow, and wrist in that order. This sequence of rotating body parts builds racket momentum as each body part extends toward the ball, one after the other. The final result is a sum of forces you would be unable to generate with just one body part and certainly not with your arm and wrist.

Make sure that you begin your serving motion deliberately and move the racket slowly throughout the backswing. As your racket arm bends at the end of the backswing, speed up the racket head as your body uncoils toward the ball. Rather than focus solely on the speed of your serve, emphasize

Figure 9.8 Lift the ball into place for your toss to produce a consistent serve.

consistency, placement, and spin. Power is the fourth component and is effective only if the other controls are well in hand.

Probably the most common barrier to a consistent serve is an erratic ball toss. For a consistent toss, hold the ball in your fingertips, not your palm. Think of lifting or placing the ball with your palm facing upward rather than tossing it. Release the ball just as your nonracket arm reaches shoulder height (figure 9.8). Aim to place the ball just above the highest point you can reach with your racket, which allows you to contact the ball just as it begins to fall.

STROKE DOCTOR

When tossing the ball for a serve, releasing it too soon will result in erratic ball placement for the hit because a slight error at release is magnified at the hitting point. Releasing too late usually results in a ball that goes backward over your head. Lifting the ball too high above your intended contact point makes it difficult for you to time the hit, especially on a windy day. To practice lifting the ball consistently, execute the full beginning of the serve. Lift the ball just above the contact point and, as it falls, catch it in your nonracket hand without striking the ball. If the ball consistently lands in your hand, your chances of hitting a successful serve are pretty good.

When receiving serve in singles, your optimal return is a forehand or backhand drive deep crosscourt or down the middle. If you can accomplish one of these strokes on most returns, you will neutralize the serve as a potential weapon. Because there is no net player to threaten a poach of your return, you should clear the net comfortably and thereby add depth to your return.

The key to consistent service returns is to watch the ball come off your opponent's racket. As soon as you determine whether the ball is coming to your forehand or backhand side, execute a unit turn of your shoulders and racket together to prepare to strike the ball. Check the timing of your unit turn on any serve that hits the net. By the time the served ball reaches the net, you should have completed the unit turn.

If your opponent hits a forceful serve, try returning from behind the baseline to give yourself more time to play the ball. Shorten your backswing and use the pace from her serve to supply the power for your return.

Two new returns to develop as a singles player are a short, angled return crosscourt and a punishing down-the-line winner or approach shot. Let's take a look at each one.

If you want to force your opponent to move forward from the baseline, chip or slice the ball with backspin short into the service box crosscourt. Chances are you'll surprise him. At the very least you will force him to move off the baseline. Because you are aiming for a short return, restrict your backswing to about half the normal length and aim lower to the net than usual.

If your opponent has a weak second serve, you have two options. First, move inside the baseline if you expect a shallow serve. If you have mastered a punishing forehand or backhand, drive it down the line and follow the flight of the ball to the net position. As an alternative, you might prefer to slice the ball and aim a deep approach shot down the line. Although you are more likely to get a return from the sliced approach, you will have gained the offensive position at the net.

RETURNING A FORCEFUL SERVE

Returning serve often requires a defensive shot, and good servers will start out most points on the offense. To counter a forceful serve, adjust your position by moving back to gain time or move in to take the ball on the rise with a shortened swing. To avoid giving up an ace, bisect the angle of possible serves. If the ball is very wide, lands on a line, or bounces unexpectedly, lob the return right down the middle of the court.

Practice Tip

Returning serve is rarely practiced as much as it deserves to be. To make it challenging, ask a practice partner to serve to you. Set up targets in the areas you want to aim to, and keep track of the number of times you can direct the ball to the target areas both short and deep. After 5 minutes, switch roles with your practice partner. To add competition, keep a tally of who can record the highest number of returns to the target areas.

Passing Shots and Lobs

A strong foundation of defensive shots is critical if your opponent likes to come to the net. A few pointers about the strategy and technique of passing shots and lobs may help.

Usually, you will want to hit a passing shot with topspin against an opponent at the net to keep the ball at your opponent's feet. Think of the passing shot as a two-shot play: hit a low crosscourt topspin shot that the net player pops up weakly, and then move in for the killing shot down the line. Alternately, you might aim down the line first to stretch him wide and then drive the ball crosscourt on the second shot. A word of caution: The net is 6 inches (15 centimeters) higher at the side, so a shot down the line is best played when you can play a ball waist high or higher. On low shots, the crosscourt shot is the better-percentage play.

Passing shots will be twice as effective if you also can threaten to lob over the net player. Just the threat prevents her from closing in to the net, and the momentary hesitation may allow your shot to get past her. Most players try to lob over the opponent's backhand side because that is a difficult shot to handle. Also consider lobbing into the sun if that is a factor. On windy days, lob against the wind, and drive when the wind is at your back to keep the ball in the court.

Lobs can be hit with backspin or topspin to control their depth. The backspin lob is better as a defensive shot and is easier to learn. The topspin lob is often a winner if you can execute it because it bounces away from the net player once it is over her head. Apply backspin when you are on defense, such as returning a smash, or are off balance, and use topspin if you are well balanced and have a ball that is comfortable to play.

Technique Adjustments for the 50-Plus Player

In chapter 8, we offered suggestions for players over 50 to counteract the likely gradual loss of various physical abilities. Most notably, muscular strength and endurance tend to decline as we age unless we train vigorously to prevent it. General body flexibility often follows a similar path. As those changes become a factor, you can adjust your tennis technique to compensate.

All stroking techniques should emphasize body and racket movements that are efficient, flowing, and relaxed. Tensing muscles, swinging too hard, and chasing after impossible winners are counterproductive in the long run. Take your time, relax, and aim for smooth movements, good balance, and anticipation of your opponent's shots.

We also suggested in chapter 8 that you shrink the size of the court by learning to play some balls from three-fourths court or midcourt. If you adopt this strategy, you'll have to practice taking balls out of the air by hitting low volleys and half-volleys. To take a ball out of the air at waist height or above, use a medium-length swing, and control it by applying spin to the ball. A full swing is unnecessary and usually a detriment because you have less time to prepare for the ball. You do not need the power of a full stroke to hit a forceful shot deep to your opponent.

Playing low balls requires a knee bend to get low to the ball. Do not bend over from the waist. Your goal is to play the ball back deep to your opponent and move closer to the net for the next shot. Control the height of the ball over the net by adjusting your racket face so that the ball clears the net but does not pop up weakly, producing an easy shot for your opponent. When playing a low ball out of the air or on the half-volley, use very little backswing, a longer follow-through to guide the ball deep, and spin to control the depth. You should also soften your hands a bit to absorb the speed of the ball because these low balls are essentially touch shots.

Perhaps the most important advice is to rely more on placement than power to win points. Once you have maneuvered your opponent into a poor court position, your winning shot should have just enough speed to get the job done with no wasted effort. Save your power shots for times when they are the only alternative.

Finally, simplifying your racket technique will produce less stress on your body and reduce the possibility of injury. An accumulation of years of serving and hitting overheads at full speed will eventually cause an overuse injury to your shoulder, elbow, or rotator cuff muscles. The following practices will help you prevent possible injuries:

- Schedule regular sessions with a certified tennis professional to improve your tennis technique by making it more sound mechanically and less stressful to your body.
- Hit more serves and overheads at three-fourths speed and aim to win points through placement rather than power.
- Engage faithfully in an off-court fitness program that improves your muscular strength, endurance, and overall flexibility to fight the aging process.

Practice Tips for Singles Play

The following practice routines are time-tested methods that focus on specific singles skills with clear objectives in mind. At their core is a common theme of developing consistency during a point, working the ball around the court, and waiting for the opportunity to take advantage of a weak shot from your opponent.

Practicing the following drills will help you prevent unforced errors and keep you in a competitive match against any player at your level of play.

- **Rally test.** Because most singles play is based on your ability to rally without an error, attempt to hit at least 100 shots with a practice partner. A shot is good only if it lands behind the service line in the deep part of the court. As you gain skill, count only shots that land in the back half of the backcourt.

- **Three-shot tennis.** Isolate the serve, return, and first shot. Many shots end before those three shots are played, so work on hitting those patterns consistently.

- **Work the point.** To learn to work your way into a point, agree with a practice partner that the ball must cross the net three times before the point even begins. An error on one of the first three shots means you have to replay the point.

- **21 points.** Eliminate the serve and return. Play a baseline game that begins with one player putting the ball in play from the baseline with a groundstroke. As the rally develops, either player may approach the net to win the point. Play until one player earns 21 points and switch who starts the play every 5 points; this is similar to table tennis.

- **Offense–defense.** One player is the retriever and one is the offensive player. The offensive player moves the retriever around the court by varying the speed, spin, and direction of every shot. The retriever pushes every ball back to the middle. Switch roles after an appropriate time.

- **Weak-serve attack.** Learn to attack a weak second serve. Agree with a practice partner to play a set in which both players get only one serve that must be struck underhand. In all other ways it is a normal set. The receiving player must attack the weak serve and approach the net. The point continues normally until it is won or lost. In this game, the receiver should win more times than the server.

- **One-serve tennis.** In this variation of the weak-serve attack game the server is allowed to serve overhand. The pressure of hitting only one serve exposes a weak second serve, and the receiver should attack and come to the net.

- **Patterns of play.** Plot several patterns of play that you want to add to your repertoire. Practice them with the help of a cooperative partner. After 5 minutes, switch roles and let her choose a pattern to work on. For example, hit deep to one side followed by a short ball to the other, and then play the point to conclusion. The possible patterns are endless but should be based on shot sequences that you feel comfortable hitting and fit into your personal style of play.

WORDS TO THE WISE

- Note the stroke technique similarities between singles and doubles by rereading chapter 6.
- Add to your skills by understanding the differences in technique from doubles and work on adding these refinements to your shot repertoire.
- Emphasize consistency and depth on ground strokes and learn to hit topspin at least on the forehand side.
- Adjust serving and receiving skills to the strategic principles of singles and add new shots or positioning to achieve those principles.
- Learn when and how to hit down the sideline to attack a short ball or a weak serve.
- Adjust your game after age 50 by improving racket technique, relying more on placement than power, and engaging in an off-court conditioning program.
- Use modified games to practice the specific skills you need to add to be successful in singles. You can invent drills and games by imitating a typical pattern of play during a point.

Beyond the Court

Although tennis is played on a court, there is much to learn about off-court tennis as well. In this part, we focus on three primary areas: selecting the best tennis equipment, caring for and conditioning the body, and integrating tennis into your lifestyle.

The game of tennis is fun, and the hours you spend playing on the court will be some of the best of your life. However, you also need to spend time off the tennis court preparing to play. This is no different from any other avocation where people read about it, make arrangements, talk to their friends, and gather tips from professionals. Gathering information off court will ensure that the hours you spend playing will be hassle free.

The first chapter in this part deals with tennis equipment. At first blush, you may think it's all about grabbing a racket and a few tennis balls and heading out the door. But a few well-informed choices can make a huge difference in your playing experience. With all the advances in racket technology, it is easy to become overwhelmed by the choices. We'll give you the basics so you can be an informed consumer. Then you should rely on a certified tennis professional to guide you in your selection.

Equally important to your comfort are good-quality tennis shoes, a hat, and tennis clothing. New designs, fabrics, and manufacturing processes have combined to produce tennis apparel that is functional, attractive, and comfortable. Although you may not care to be a fashion plate on the court, using good sense in apparel choices will enhance your experience and possibly improve your play.

In chapter 2, we discussed the innumerable physical benefits of tennis. At the same time, we warned that your personal health and fitness cannot be at an optimal level if you only play tennis. In chapter 11, we'll take a look at the critical areas of warming up before play and cooling down afterward. We'll also consider the importance of off-court training for strength, flexibility, and balance to ensure you can play your best on the court.

Nothing is more frustrating than to be sidelined from tennis play because of an injury, whether it is an annoying temporary problem or a more serious injury that requires assistance from a health care professional. We'll help you devise a logical action plan to deal with typical overuse injuries common to tennis players. In many cases, choosing court surfaces that are kinder to your body can prevent injuries. We'll also give you advice on the best types of courts to play on.

In chapter 12, we'll suggest options and alternatives for keeping the passion for the sport alive. Even if you have played tennis all of your life, keeping it new, fresh, and exciting takes planning and smart choices. Millions of people have played tennis at some point in their lives but stopped playing. Their reasons reveal common themes that you can combat with smart planning and organization. We'll suggest ways to expand your circle of tennis friends and partners, test yourself in new situations, and create new adventures and experiences to add zest to your personal tennis lifestyle.

No More Wooden Rackets

Amazing design, production, and manufacturing advances in tennis rackets have been made in the last 20 years. Gone are the bulky, unwieldy, wooden frames and presses and fragile strings. Today's racket frames are made of aluminum, sometimes in combination with titanium or magnesium.

Other composite rackets are made with various combinations of boron, graphite, or ceramic. Rackets are about the same length, but they are lighter, stronger, and stiffer and have significantly larger heads. Larger racket heads with expanded sweet spots increase the odds that players make contact in the center of the strings, producing more consistent shots. All those factors add up to make it easier to hit the ball accurately with more spin and pace. Sounds good doesn't it?

In this chapter, we focus on the tools of the trade of tennis equipment in general. Our reach includes rackets, shoes, and clothing. In each area, we give you key advice in selecting the optimal equipment and point out the potential benefits. Specifically, we cover selecting a tennis racket, choosing the right strings, obtaining tennis balls, selecting the best tennis shoes and clothing, and packing your bag.

Tennis Rackets

If you want a picture of the changes in tennis during the past 25 years, check out a video of a professional match played in the 1970s or early 1980s. The players appear to be pushing the ball back and forth across the net compared to today's play. The racket technology of the past (wooden rackets) encouraged smooth, long strokes and consistency from the baseline. Today's professional players, in contrast, seem to pummel each ground stroke with an almost violent swing and exaggerated follow-through. You may not want to imitate their swing style completely, but the new racket technology will allow you to hit a tennis ball in ways that you thought were possible only in your dreams.

Let's begin with three overall recommendations for selecting the right racket. First, enlist a knowledgeable teaching professional to help you through the process. Second, try several demo rackets, which are available at most shops, to see how you like the racket before you invest any money. Third, if you ask for help from a teaching professional and use his or her demo racket, please purchase a racket from that person rather than heading out to the chain sporting goods store to save a few bucks.

The most popular racket manufacturers in the United States have consistently been Prince, Wilson, and Head. Each of these companies offers a wide range of rackets with different playing characteristics and in various price ranges. You can't go wrong with a racket from these leading manufacturers. Other brands produce good-quality rackets as well, but they are less well known and command a smaller market share.

Next, let's look at grip size. There are two common methods for determining your optimal grip size. For the first method, use a ruler to measure the distance from the tip of your ring finger on your racket hand to the farthest main

Get professional advice when choosing a new racket.

vertical line in you hand (figure 10.1a). This measurement typically shows a grip size of 4 1/4, 4 3/8, 4 1/2, 4 5/8, or 4 3/4 inches (European sizes 2, 3, 4, 5, and 6), which are the most common grip sizes for rackets.

For the second method, hold the racket with your dominant hand and slide the index finger of the other hand between the tips of your fingers and the base of your palm (figure 10.1b). If the grip is too small, there will be no room for the index finger. If there is extra room, the grip is too large.

Most men have a grip size between 4 1/2 and 4 3/4 inches (European size 4 to 6). For women, the range is typically 4 1/8 to 4 1/2 (European size 1 to 4). Keep in mind that if you add an overgrip for cushioning or absorbing perspiration, it will increase your grip size by about 1/8 inch (one European size).

Choose a grip size that is comfortable. Keep in mind, however, that a grip that is too large will force you to squeeze the racket more tightly and tire your arm. At the opposite extreme, a small grip may cause you to whip the racket and eventually cause arm or elbow problems. Try a racket with the grip size indicated by your measurement and use it for a while. If it feels uncomfortable, experiment with one size larger or smaller.

Today's rackets are made of aluminum or a composite of several materials, such as boron or graphite. A beginning player on a limited budget will

a   b

Figure 10.1   Determining grip size: *(a)* ruler technique; *(b)* racket technique.

probably be happy with a prestrung aluminum racket in the price range of $75 to $125. After some time, you may want to upgrade to a higher-performance racket, which may cost about double the price. If you choose a higher-performance racket, buy it unstrung and put in the strings that you find most playable.

Customized Rackets

Customize your racket by determining your style of game and matching it to the recommendations of the manufacturer. Independent evaluations of all the major rackets appear annually in *Tennis* magazine, which is available at newsstands. Typically, style of play is described as *power* (long, looping swings), *finesse* (short, compact swings), or *combination* (varied shots and skills that compromise between power and control).

Power players are more likely to choose midsized or traditional-sized racket heads, which create less resistance as they move through the air, allowing the player to generate more power. Most players on the professional tour use this size head. Rackets with oversized heads typically range from 110 to 125 square inches (710 to 806 square centimeters), while midsized rackets are about 100 to 109 square inches (645 to 703 square centimeters). Traditional rackets have heads smaller than 100 square inches (645 square centimeters). Oversized heads are most popular with

Traditional, midsized, and oversized racket heads.

recreational players because they have a larger sweet spot, which allows a greater margin for error on off-center hits. Most players over 50 would probably benefit from playing with a mid- or oversized racket head.

Finesse players typically look for a stiffer racket frame to provide more power and a larger head to increase the sweet spot. The manufacturer or a tennis magazine report will list each racket's comparative stiffness based on playing tests. More flexible racket frames are more forgiving, particularly on off-center hits. If you suffer from arm or shoulder pain, a flexible racket frame may be helpful because the frame absorbs some of the shock of the ball contact.

Combination players seek both power and control. Their racket choices are more individualized because they may want to emphasize control on some shots and power on others. Generally, these players choose mid- or oversized racket heads and fairly stiff frames. If they seek power on the serve, they may choose rackets that are lighter in the head. Those who rely on powerful ground strokes may choose heavier rackets.

Length, Weight, and Balance

Most rackets are 27 to 28 inches (69 to 71 centimeters) long from the tip to the butt of the handle. Although some models are available in longer lengths, few players have found them to be effective because they lack maneuverability.

Racket weight can vary considerably. A heavy racket weighs more than 11 ounces (312 grams), midweight rackets weigh between 9.8 and 10.9 ounces (278 to 309 grams), and superlight rackets weigh between 9 and 9.4 ounces (255 to 266 grams). Generally, heavier rackets produce more power, less torque, and better control. However, the tradeoff is that they require more muscular strength to manipulate. Over the course of a match, a heavier racket may contribute to overall fatigue.

Older players will enjoy the increased maneuverability of lighter rackets along with increased power and spin. Lighter rackets are also more suitable for doubles players because the emphasis in doubles is on serves, returns, volleys, and overheads. Heavier rackets have more value for singles players who want to generate maximum power on baseline ground strokes.

Tennis rackets are described as either *balanced, head heavy,* or *head light.* Theoretically, a lighter head allows you to whip the racket faster while serving. A more balanced racket might work better on baseline shots. However, you need to consider all of the factors—overall weight, head size, length, and balance—to appreciate how a racket performs. Manufacturers constantly tinker with these factors to produce the best playing characteristics. Most players simply play test rackets until they find one that feels good to them.

You really do need to have at least two identical rackets available every time you play. If you break a string or otherwise damage the racket, you'll want an identical substitute. While you have new strings put in, you'll also have an available racket.

Racket Strings

Most less-expensive tennis rackets come prestrung from the manufacturer at medium string tensions with durable strings. As you raise your level of play, you'll want to purchase your rackets unstrung and customize your strings to your playing style.

Natural gut used to be the premier string for serious tennis players even though it didn't last long and was susceptible to moisture. These days, synthetic strings are made of high-quality materials that are durable and provide a great feel. The only factors you need to consider are the gauge, or thickness, of the strings and the tension at which to string them.

The number 15, 16, or 17 identifies the gauge of strings. The lower-number gauge is a thicker string and therefore more durable. The higher-gauge string clearly has a better feel on the ball but tends not to last as long. Experiment with different types of strings and gauges to determine your preferences.

String tension is recommended by every manufacturer for each racket and is usually found stamped on the throat. Follow those recommendations and adjust them to your own preference. Tighter strings provide better control because there is less give in the strings at ball contact. Looser strings provide more power. If you have arm, elbow, or shoulder problems, use looser strings and let the racket do the work.

Plan to restring your racket every few months to maximize performance. A general guide is that if you play three times per week, your racket should be restrung at least three times in a calendar year. Of course, if you break a string, you have to have it restrung. If you apply heavy spin to your shots, you're more likely to break strings. Over time, strings will lose tension. If you keep playing with older strings until they break, you'll probably find more shots flying over the baseline from your loose strings.

Tennis Balls

Three tennis balls cost about $3 today, or a dollar a ball. The cost was the same 25 years ago. What other item can you think of that is the same price today as 25 years ago? What a great bargain!

Most serious tennis players open a new can of balls each time they play. The cost split among four doubles players is relatively minor. Keep used tennis balls around for practice or for your kids to use, or donate them to the tennis facility to use in instructional programs.

Tennis ball packages should state that the enclosed tennis balls are approved by the United States Tennis Association or the International Tennis Federation. This means that they have been tested for size, weight, rebound, and deformation. There are slightly modified balls for playing at altitude (above 4,000 feet [1,219 meters]) and different balls for hard and soft courts.

The most popular brands in the United States are Penn and Wilson. Other brands such as Dunlop and Slazenger are more popular in other countries. Prince has also begun to manufacture tennis balls that have excellent playability.

Most serious tennis players open a new can of tennis balls for each match.

Interestingly, there has been much experimentation with tennis balls to control the speed of the game in the past 10 years. Although the jury is still out for professional tennis, beginning players and kids definitely benefit from playing with a slower, low-compression ball that allows more time to get into hitting position. If you hit with young grandchildren, start with balloons, move up to foam balls, and then use slower-bouncing transition or low-compression balls. (The lower bounce allows a child to contact the ball at a more comfortable height.) Most sporting goods stores carry these types or you can check the Internet.

Tennis Shoes

Feet are amazing. Do you know that one foot and ankle is composed of 26 bones, 33 joints, and more than a hundred muscles, tendons, and ligaments that hold everything together? No wonder things go wrong.

Equally amazing is what we expect of our feet. A 200-pound (90.7-kilogram) man lands with up to 600 pounds (272 kilograms) of force on each foot several thousand times during a leisurely jog. Imagine the stress on your feet during a few sets of tennis with all the starts, stops, twists, and turns. Although well-worn tennis shoes may feel comfortable, they won't do much to relieve the stress on your feet, and your safety may be compromised by lack of support or court traction.

When you buy tennis shoes, the main considerations in order of importance should be safety and comfort. Wrong choices will put your feet at risk of injuries that could end your tennis career or at least make you miserable. The agony of "defeet" can be much worse than losing a tennis match.

Over time our feet become more prone to injuries because of age and overuse. We may have abused them for years and gotten away with it, but there comes a time when the sins of the past catch up. Seek the help of a health care professional such as a podiatrist if you have foot problems. A professional can assess your foot problems, recommend the type of shoe you should buy, prescribe orthotics if necessary, and prescribe exercises to improve strength and flexibility.

Let's start with safety considerations. Buy tennis shoes to play tennis and forget running shoes or cross-trainers. Unlike other athletic shoes, tennis shoes are built to provide the lateral support that the game requires. Court shoes today are designed with thinner midsoles to bring players closer to the court while still providing good cushioning. The thinner midsole helps lower the center of gravity and reduces the side-to-side ankle motion.

Another safety factor is the type of sole and the friction it creates with the court surface. Tennis shoes for clay courts have a herringbone design that does not absorb clay granules and allows you to slide into or out of a shot. Hard-court shoes are more durable and need to cushion your feet from the pounding they take on harder surfaces. You may have to experiment on your own when choosing a shoe that works on the courts where you play most often. All hard and soft courts do not play the same. How a court plays depends largely on the surface design and texture.

Comfort in tennis shoes is nearly as important as injury prevention. A lack of comfort signals that something is not quite right. Find someone to help you determine whether your foot plant is supinated (the feet roll outward), which causes wear on the outside of the shoes; pronated (the feet roll inward), which causes wear on the inside of the shoes; or ideal, which causes even wear. Pronated feet suffer the most from overuse injuries, and each type of foot reacts better to shoes designed for that type of foot. Some higher-end sporting shoe stores employ people knowledgeable in this area who can help you make a wise choice.

You need a half-inch to an inch (1.3 to 2.5 centimeters) of space between your longest toe and the end of the shoe. The frequent forward-and-back moves in tennis often produce what is called *tennis toe* from the repetitive jamming of the toes into the end of the shoe when you stop suddenly. The heel of the shoe should be snug, although you need a small amount of movement. Keep in mind that your foot will swell during the day, so the size must be able to accommodate that change. You may want to purchase tennis shoes a half or full size larger than normal to accommodate foot swelling or provide room for heavy athletic socks.

Tennis shoes should be sturdy but lightweight to prevent fatigue. Depending on the climate in which you play, the upper part of the shoe can be mesh, leather, or canvas. Mesh shoes breathe better in warm climates and dry more quickly, but leather shoes will stretch with your foot. If you live in heat and humidity, like we do in Florida, it's a good idea to rotate two pairs of shoes to allow them to dry thoroughly between days of play.

Don't chuckle, but some people like us have injured our feet by tying the laces too tight. We've learned the hard way that you can reduce the pressure on your foot and enlarge the width of your shoes by using just every other eyelet. You might also consider round shoelaces to better distribute the pressure across the top of your feet.

Try on new tennis shoes in a store and break them in before you play. Internet shopping and mail-order catalogs can save you money once you know the exact shoe you need, but are risky alternatives without a test drive in new shoes.

All this advice may seem to be overkill, but we all know people who blame their shoes for unstable ankles, sprains, blisters, calluses, shin splints, Achilles rupture, heel and arch pain, ingrown toenails, corns, bunions, and just plan aching feet. It's much better to be smart in picking the right shoes in the first place. Your feet will thank you.

Clothing

Shopping for tennis clothing used to be easy. You just shopped for white. But times have changed, and tennis clothes now span the spectrum of colors, styles, and fabrics.

The best thing about today's tennis clothing is that cotton fabrics have been replaced by polyesters such as Coolmax and Wickaway, which breathe and help you stay cool and dry, even in the heat of the summer. Along with their utilitarian function of cooling, today's fabrics are also more durable. In fact, many styles of tennis clothing are so adaptable that you may find you like to wear them off the court, too.

Tennis warm-ups are a must for most of the year to keep your muscles warm before and after play. Hats are mandatory to combat the rays of the summer sun and offer protection for the eyes, hair, and scalp. Wristbands collect perspiration from the arms and help you hold onto your grip.

Styles of tennis clothes change constantly. Tennis dresses go in and out of style, tennis skirts are classic, and tennis shorts for women work for some players. Tennis skirts with build-in compression shorts are popular since they

Tennis clothes should be comfortable, practical, and stylish.

address modesty concerns and feel more comfortable to many women. Sports bras are equally popular for the same reasons.

Men's tennis clothing fashions are more stable, although the length of shorts has certainly increased. Don't you love those old clips of McEnroe, Borg, and Connors in their short shorts? Perhaps the most notable fashion change has been toward collar-less shirts. It used to be taboo to appear without a collar, and shirt-tails had to be tucked in. Today's fashion dictates no collar and shirts are designed to be worn out. These changes are sensible and much more comfortable.

One final piece of advice. If you are invited to play at a new tennis facility, check the cloth-ing restrictions. Some places still allow only white tennis clothing.

Packing Your Bag

This may seem like a silly section. Shouldn't you already know what you'll need to pack for a tennis match? Well, we've learned a lot from other play-ers over the years, and while we like to travel light, we have found some helpful suggestions. Here are essential items we think you should pack for every match.

The most important accoutrement is a bottle and water or sports drink to ensure that you have adequate fluid during and after play. Another critical item is a snack bar or fruit in case you need refueling during or just after play. Other items include the following:

- A second racket
- A new can of tennis balls
- Practice balls for warm-up

- Wristbands
- A towel for use during play
- A hat or visor
- Sunscreen
- Contact lenses, glasses, and sunglasses
- First aid supplies such as athletic tape and adhesive bandages, ice bags, anti-inflammatory medication, and aspirin
- Products that help you grip the racket in heat and humidity
- A change of shirt or clothing for after play
- Warm-ups or a sweater for after play
- A towel and toiletries for an after-play shower
- Other personal items
- Telephone numbers of playing partners (stored in mobile phone)

You may need additional items specific to the climate, time of year, indoor or outdoor play, and the distance from your home. Your tennis facility might have a pro shop where emergency purchases can be made if you forget something. We've shown up to play lacking shoes, socks, shorts, towels, and unmentionables—not all on the same occasion at least.

WORDS TO THE WISE

- Ask for professional help when selecting a racket and play-test several before you decide.
- Keep your racket strings fresh, and choose a type that enhances your style of game.
- Choose the right tennis shoes by emphasizing safety first and then comfort.
- Get in style with new tennis clothing fabrics, colors, and design that are both practical and comfortable.
- Pack your tennis bag carefully.

Body Talk

Tennis players tend to focus on their strokes and skills or their ability to compete. But if you really want to enjoy tennis for years to come, change your focus by zeroing in on caring for your body. Even elite, competitive players, who tend to be much younger, typically adopt this practice after learning the hard way.

In our younger years, we generally didn't have to be so conscious of our bodies and just expected that they would perform on demand. But with the aging process, we naturally lose strength, endurance, and flexibility unless we counteract this trend with an intelligent fitness regimen. One of the best things we can do to protect our bodies is to choose the best playing surface available.

The right court surface will ease the shock on your body and minimize the chance of injury. Soft clay-based or composition court surfaces provide natural cushioning from the frequent stops and starts of tennis play. The newer, cushioned hard courts provide much of the same comfort and require less water and maintenance than clay courts.

In general, you'll find better courts and more user-friendly courts at commercial and private tennis facilities. Tennis courts built at public schools and most parks are often made from the most economical materials. You may be saving money playing at those facilities, but you're also punishing your body. At our age, who needs it? Find a court with a soft surface and stick to it if you can. Your bones, muscles, and joints will say, "Thank you!"

Preventing injuries is better than dealing with them. For example, many players choose to wear a knee brace.

The more you play tennis, the more likely it is that you'll face myriad annoying strains, sprains, and minor injuries that can detract from your enjoyment of the game. The worst scenario is being forced to give up tennis for extended periods and perhaps becoming fearful of resuming play even when you are healthy again.

Although tennis is a relatively safe sport compared to many others, the demands on your body are considerable. The quick stops and starts, constant short bursts, and repetition of identical movements can lead to overuse or traumatic injuries. Of course, if your level of endurance is not adequate, you risk injuries if your body is not up to the physical demands of play over extended periods. This chapter addresses tennis technique and its impact on the body; the importance of warming up before play and cooling down after; ways to build strength, improve flexibility, and improve and maintain dynamic balance; when to seek the advice of health care professionals; how to fuel your body for exercise; and how to prevent and care for injuries.

Tennis Technique and the Body

Watch a competent senior player on the court. Typically, he will use sound technique that minimizes the shock to his body. Grips, swings, and court movement will be efficient and measured and seemingly require little effort.

Let's look at a common example of how tennis technique affects the body. A common problem for many players is the grip on the backhand side. If your hand is in front of the racket (figure 11.1*a*) rather than on top and behind, your arm and shoulder will absorb the shock of the ball hitting

a   b

Figure 11.1 *(a)* Backhand grip with poor support; *(b)* backhand grip with proper support.

your racket. You would be much better off changing to a grip that puts your hand, arm, and shoulder behind the racket at the point of contact with the ball (figure 11.1*b*), thereby eliminating the shock. It is simply a matter of using the laws of physics to support the racket and ball impact in the proper position. Another possibility is to convert to a two-handed backhand, using the nonracket hand for support behind the racket.

Here is another example from the serve. Many players face the net or open their body too soon during the serve (figure 11.2*a*). The result is that most of the power is supplied by the arm and shoulder rather than from the legs upward followed by a rotation of the large muscles of the hips, trunk, and upper body. Eventually, the arm will become fatigued, and overuse will put inordinate strain on the serving arm or on the rotator cuff muscles of the shoulder area. If you keep using that same serve, an overuse injury will be the likely result, possibly leading to surgery. Keep your shoulders sideways until the racket has actually moved into the hitting area of the serve, and let your body naturally follow the racket (figure 11.2*b*).

On the forehand side, a late contact point and failure to use the upper-body rotation to supply power puts tremendous stress on the racket arm (figure 11.3*a*). At the point of impact, your racket hand and arm should be even with your front foot, using a square stance. There is about a 45-degree angle between the shoulder of your racket arm and the contact point, which

a   b

Figure 11.2 *(a)* **Player opens shoulders too soon on serve;** *(b)* **player's body opens correctly by following the racket path.**

provides leverage against the oncoming ball. A late contact point, which might be anywhere from your belt buckle to your back, puts your arm in a weak position. Trying to use your arm to muscle the shot rather than rotating your shoulders and hips into the shot magnifies the stress on your arm. The solution for a late contact point is to prepare earlier, begin your forward swing a bit earlier, and aim for contact in line with your front foot. As your racket moves forward, allow your hips and upper body to rotate naturally to follow your racket and generate racket speed (figure 11.3*b*).

These scenarios are typical issues for tennis players. The good news is that they can be avoided by developing and practicing sound body mechanics

a   b

Figure 11.3 *(a)* Late contact on forehand and no trunk rotation; *(b)* proper contact point and body rotation.

through proper tennis technique. A certified, experienced teaching professional can help you prevent these types of problems. Seek counsel and periodically spend time improving your skills under the watchful eye of a trusted coach. It will be well worth your while to make the investment in order to prevent body aches and pains caused by poor or flawed tennis technique.

Female players will likely take these suggestions to heart and schedule time with a trusted coach. Male players, well that's another story. Many male tennis players consider themselves to be at least somewhat athletic and are self-taught players for the most part. They pick up ideas from each other, watch professional players, and develop their own style of play. When they have time to play tennis, they want to play and compete rather than take a lesson.

The problem with this approach is that technique errors become magnified over time as the body ages. Players become more susceptible to injury and require longer recovery time. Guys, just swallow your pride and schedule some time with a coach. We promise you that you'll love learning to play better and you'll forestall most overuse injuries.

When you do consult a coach, make sure you have an idea what your trouble spots are. If you are not sure, explain that you would like your coach to evaluate your overall game and then together make a plan for technique adjustments.

You may wonder how often you should consult a coach for help on technique. Any professional can help you best by spending time with you several times per year. Just like you schedule checkups with your physician, dentist, ophthalmologist, and others, pencil in your teaching professional. At a minimum, consider a couple of lessons at the start of each season of play.

We should qualify these recommendations by saying that they are intended for improving tennis technique. If you enjoy playing competitively and want to improve your ability as a competitor or expand your understanding of strategy and tactics, add coaching for those purposes to the mix. The best arrangement for those types of coaching is in a group or team situation, which makes them more fun and affordable.

Here is a final word about the contribution a good coach can make to your game: If you ask for an overall tune-up or evaluation of your game, also ask an experienced coach for an evaluation of your overall body strength, flexibility, and dynamic balance. She will quickly spot how you move to the ball, accelerate your racket, react to forced emergency situations, and whether your body and racket movements are efficient. Help her by explaining that you are concerned not only about your racket work, but also how your body functions on the court.

All players benefit from the advice and encouragement of a good coach.

Warming Up Before Play

Before playing, almost all tennis players use a traditional warm-up, which consists of rallying from the backcourt, hitting a few volleys and overheads from the net, and serving for several minutes. Although this may help prepare you to play, these activities do little for your body. A better idea is to warm up your body before you ever hit a shot and help prepare it for the physical stress that it is about to face.

Research has demonstrated that dynamic stretching—stretching with movement—is the best preparation for play, and the movements you make should mimic those that will occur during play. Avoid sudden, jerky movements. If you feel pain, stop and seek medical attention. As with any exercise program, consult your physician before beginning.

Begin with about 5 minutes of overall general body warm-up. Try walking, light jogging, jumping jacks, or side-shuffling. Riding a stationary bike or walking on a treadmill are also excellent general warm-up activities. The objective of the general warm-up is to raise your body temperature, get your blood flowing to your muscles, and prepare your heart and lungs for strenuous play. At normal temperatures, you should just begin to perspire after the warm-up.

Next, you are ready for dynamic stretches. The following stretches are recommended by the Sport Science Committee of the United States Tennis Association as the best stretches before tennis play. Optimally, you should do all of these exercises before you play tennis.

LOWER-BODY STRETCHES

Toe-and-Heel Walks   This exercise targets the muscles of the calf and lower leg. Walk on your toes across the court (figure 11.4a). Repeat, walking on your heels (figure 11.4b).

Straight-Leg March   This exercise targets the hamstrings and the hip muscles. Put your arms straight out in front of you at shoulder height. With your knees straight, lift one leg toward your hands as high as you can (figure 11.5) without discomfort until you feel a stretch in the back of the leg. March from singles sideline to singles sideline and back while maintaining good balance.

All stretches are courtesy of the Sport Science Committee of the United States Tennis Association, adapted by permission of USTA. Adapted from *A Coaches' Guide and Curriculum for 50+ Tennis Players*, 2005, USTA.

a   b

Figure 11.4   *(a)* Walking on toes; *(b)* walking on heels.

Figure 11.5   Straight-leg march.

Alternating Toe Touch   This exercise targets the hamstrings and the hip muscles. Stand at the singles sideline (figure 11.6a) and step forward with the left leg, keeping the knee straight but not locked. With your right hand, reach down toward the left foot as far as is comfortable (figure 11.6b) to the point of feeling a light stretch in the back of your leg. If possible, touch your left foot. Stand up all the way, step forward with the right leg and reach for the right foot with the left hand. Walk around the court, alternately reaching for the left foot with the right hand and reaching for the right foot with the left hand. Be sure to stand up all the way between each step.

a   b

Figure 11.6   Alternating toe touch: *(a)* stand at the singles sideline; *(b)* step forward and reach toward left foot.

Figure 11.7 **Long walks.**

Long Walks This exercise targets the hip flexors and the quadriceps. Long walking is walking with extra long steps. While walking, keep your back leg nearly straight and move the hips forward until you feel a light stretch at the front of the hip on the same side as your back leg (figure 11.7). Stretch both right and left hip flexors and quadriceps by walking from singles sideline to singles sideline and back.

Forward Hurdle Walk This exercise targets the muscles of the inner and outer thighs. Move your right leg backward, up, and around to the front as if you were stepping over a hurdle that is approximately waist high (figure 11.8). While alternating legs, walk from singles sideline to singles sideline.

Figure 11.8 **Forward hurdle walk.**

Walking Side Hip Stretch This exercise targets the muscles of the outer thigh. Face the net. Cross your left leg over your right leg and push out the right hip until you feel a light stretch in the outside of your hip (figure 11.9). Stand up straight and step to the right with your right foot. Repeat, walking sideways. When you reach the singles sideline, reverse the movement, stepping to the left until you reach the left singles sideline.

UPPER-BODY STRETCHES

Forward and Backward Arm Circles This exercise targets the deltoids and the rotator cuff of the shoulder. Hold out your arms to your sides at shoulder height, palms down. Rotate your arms in small forward circles about 6 inches (15 centimeters) in diameter (figure 11.10a). Perform 10 forward circles and 10

Figure 11.9 **Walking side hip stretch.**

backward circles. Then do 10 forward and 10 backward large arm circles, using the shoulders' full range of motion (figure 11.10b). You should feel a slight stretch in the shoulders as you perform the exercise.

a   *b*

Figure 11.10 Forward and backward arm circles: *(a)* small circles; *(b)* large circles.

90/90 Internal and External Rotation This exercise targets the rotator cuff of the shoulder. With your arms out to your sides at shoulder height, bend the elbows 90 degrees so your fingers point up toward the sky. Using the shoulders' full range of motion, rotate your shoulders forward once and then backward once in a controlled manner (figure 11.11). Do 10 repetitions.

a   b

Figure 11.11   90/90 internal and external rotation: *(a)* rotate forward; *(b)* rotate backward.

Wrist Circles This exercise targets the wrist flexors and extensors in the forearm. Hold both arms out in front of your body at shoulder height, palms facing down. Rotate your wrists in clockwise circles (figure 11.12). Use the full range of motion in the wrists when performing the circles so you feel a slight stretch in the forearm muscles. Perform 10 clockwise circles. Reverse and rotate your wrists in counterclockwise circles. Do 10 repetitions.

Figure 11.12   Wrist circles.

Wrist Flexion and Extension   This exercise targets the wrist flexors and extensors in the forearm. Stand with both arms in front of your body at shoulder height. Alternately flex and extend the wrists in a controlled manner. When flexing (figure 11.13*a*), bend the hands toward the body. When extending (figure 11.13*b*), extend them away from the body. Use the complete range of motion in the wrists so that you feel a stretch in the forearm muscles. You should feel the stretch in the back of the forearms as you flex your wrists and in the front of the forearms as you extend your wrists. Do 10 repetitions, alternating between flexion and extension.

a   *b*

Figure 11.13   Wrist flexion and extension: *(a)* flexion; *(b)* extension.

TORSO STRETCHES

Standing Trunk Rotations   This exercise targets the abdominal and lower back muscles. Stand with your feet shoulder-width apart and your hands on your hips. Rotate your torso by leaning forward from the waist then moving to the right, to the back, and to the left (figure 11.14, *a* and *b*). Do 10 repetitions at a speed and range of motion that is comfortable. Reverse the direction by moving first to the front then to the left, to the back, and to the right for 10 repetitions.

a   b

Figure 11.14   **Standing trunk rotations: *(a)* lean forward from the waist; *(b)* move torso to the right.**

Diagonal Chops   This exercise targets the abdominal and lower back muscles. Stand up straight with your feet shoulder-width apart. Hold your arms together in front of you at shoulder height. Link your hands and make a chopping movement as if swinging an ax as you rotate your body to the left and bring your hands down to the left of your legs (figure 11.15, *a* and *b*). Stand up straight and repeat to the right side of the body. Perform 10 repetitions of one chop to the left and one to the right.

a   *b*

Figure 11.15 **Diagonal chops:** *(a)* **stand straight, arms together;** *(b)* **bring hands down to the left.**

Once you have completed the general body warm-up and the dynamic stretches, you are ready for the more formal warming up of your shots on the court. If your court time is limited, complete your warm-up and stretching off the tennis court to maximize your playing time.

Cooling Down After Play

Most tennis players are beginning to see the benefits of the prematch warm-up and stretching, but the number of players who actually cool down correctly is embarrassingly low. As we age, the cool-down ritual becomes more critical than ever because it allows our bodies to get rid of lactic acid and other waste products while gradually reducing the body's core temperature and heart rate. The benefit of a cool-down ritual is reduced stiffness and soreness the next day, something all of us can appreciate.

Begin your cool-down ritual by incorporating some of the same exercises or exercises similar to those suggested for the dynamic warm-up. After a few minutes, switch to the static stretches described in this section. These static stretches along with others can also be part of your regular flexibility training, which is discussed later in this chapter.

Hold a static stretch at the point of stretch, but not pain, for 15 to 30 seconds. Be sure to inhale and exhale slowly to help lower your heart rate as you stretch. Also make certain to do all the stretches on both sides of your body. You may be most comfortable stretching on the ground or floor so that you can relax and isolate the muscle being stretched.

If you spend 5 to 10 minutes after playing tennis alternating static stretching with relaxation exercises, your body will recover faster and the postmatch stiffness will nearly disappear. If you have access to a swimming pool, you might enjoy stretching in the water, which has therapeutic benefits.

STATIC STRETCHES

Knee–Chest Flex   From a standing position, bend one leg and grasp it with both hands clamped just below the knee. Slowly pull the knee to your chest (figure 11.16). Hold this position for 15 to 30 seconds.

Figure 11.16   Knee–chest flex.

All stretches are courtesy of the Sport Science Committee of the United States Tennis Association, adapted by permission of USTA. Adapted from *A Coaches' Guide and Curriculum for 50+ Tennis Players*, 2005, USTA.

Hamstring Stretch   Lie on your back and bend both knees. Straighten one leg and raise it toward the trunk. Use your hands to gently increase the stretch. Point your toes toward your face to stretch the calf (figure 11.17).

Figure 11.17   **Hamstring stretch.**

Figure-4 Hamstring Stretch   From a sitting position, place the right foot against the inside of the left knee. Try to bring the chest to the thigh by bending forward from the hips (figure 11.18). Keep the back straight. Point your toes back toward your face.

Figure 11.18   **Figure-4 hamstring stretch.**

Spinal Twist From a sitting position, place the left foot on the outside of the right knee. Bring the right arm around the left knee, resting the elbow above the outside of the left knee. Slowly turn the head and upper body to the left (figure 11.19). You'll wind up looking over your left shoulder.

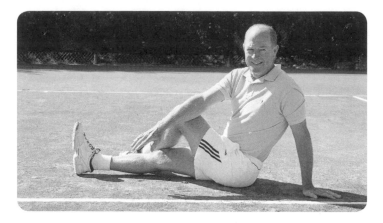

Figure 11.19 Spinal twist.

Quadriceps Stork Stretch Place one hand on a wall or post to the side of you for support, if necessary. Stand on one leg. Bend the opposite knee while grasping the ankle. Keeping the back straight and buttocks tucked under, bring your knee down as far as you can, trying to point it straight down to the ground (figure 11.20). Do not turn out the knee or twist it.

Figure 11.20 Quadriceps stork stretch.

Groin Stretch   Stand with legs greater than shoulder-width apart. Place one hand above the knee, the other hand on the opposite hip. With toes pointed forward, slowly bend the knee your hand is on until you feel a stretch in the groin area (figure 11.21). Roll your weight onto the inside of your foot. Repeat to the other side.

Figure 11.21   Groin stretch.

Hip Stretch   Stand with your left hand on a wall, your weight on your left leg, and your right leg crossed in front of it. Gently push the left hip toward the wall (figure 11.22). Increase the stretch by standing farther from the wall.

Figure 11.22   Hip stretch.

Shoulder Stretch Hold a racket in your right hand. Hold the racket behind your back by the throat or the handle; the head of the racket is pointing down. With your left hand, slowly pull the racket head down, bringing your right elbow to your ear and pointing it to the sky (figure 11.23). Then slowly pull up with the right arm, pointing the lower elbow to the floor.

Figure 11.23   Shoulder stretch.

Figure 11.24   Calf stretch.

Calf Stretch Place both hands on a wall in front of you. Extend one leg behind you, while keeping the other forward. Keep the knee of the back leg straight, the heel on the floor, and the foot pointing forward. Bend the knee of the forward leg and lean your trunk forward. Do not arch the lower back. Then slightly bend the back leg, raise the heel 2 inches (5.1 centimeters) off the floor, and lean into the wall (figure 11.24). This time, feel the stretch near the heel.

Forearm Stretch Extend one arm straight in front of you with the palm up. Use the opposite hand to gently stretch the wrist back (extension) (figure 11.25a). Turn the palm down and gently stretch the wrist downward (flexion) (figure 11.25b).

a b

Figure 11.25 Forearm stretch: *(a)* extension; *(b)* flexion.

Strength Training for Tennis

We might as well give it to you straight. There's good news and bad news about your body's strength capabilities after age 50. First the bad news, muscular strength decreases approximately 30 percent on average between the ages of 50 and 70, with even more dramatic losses after age 80. The greatest loss of muscular strength is in the lower extremities: in the muscles of the back, buttocks, thighs, and calves.

We have two primary types of muscle fibers, usually referred to as slow-twitch and fast-twitch fibers. Slow-twitch muscle fibers are slow to contract, slow to fatigue, and provide muscular endurance. Fast-twitch fibers contract quickly and help us accelerate movements, but they tend to tire quickly. As we age, we experience a 25 to 50 percent reduction in the number and size of fast-twitch fibers, especially in the back, thighs (quadriceps and hamstrings), and calves.

So what does this mean? It means that without intervention, age will diminish your muscle mass, explosiveness, speed, and jumping ability.

Now the good news. Through strength and resistance training you can reverse the aging process and significantly reduce your loss of strength. Through strength training, you will also improve bone health, posture, and flexibility; decrease body fat; and increase metabolism. It's a great deal.

Resistance training is overloading your muscles by placing increasing demands on them to stress them beyond their accustomed loads. This does not mean you have to join a gym or spend hours lifting weights. You can overload your muscles using your body weight, resistance bands or elastic tubing, free weights or food cans of different sizes, medicine or stability balls, and fixed weights on a machine.

The key is to get coaching from a knowledgeable, certified strength trainer who understands your goals and understands that you want to increase your overall body strength to help you play tennis and prevent injury. Once you have a program in place, you can perform the exercises at home and consult your trainer occasionally to assess your progress and perhaps add new exercises for variety or increase the number of sets, repetitions, or amount of resistance. If you prefer to do research on your own, try *Strength Training Past 50* by Wayne L. Westcott and Thomas R. Baechle (Human Kinetics, 2007) or *Complete Conditioning for Tennis* by E. Paul Roetert and Todd S. Ellenbecker (Human Kinetics, 2007).

Generally, strength training should involve all the major muscle groups with particular emphasis on the key postural muscles, the muscles that hold the body erect against gravity. Specifically, these muscles support the spine, shoulders, and pelvis. The abdominal and lower back muscles are key to providing support for your spine. In addition, tennis players need to be particularly aware that injuries in tennis occur most frequently to the wrist, elbow, shoulder, lower back, hamstrings, and calf. Make sure your exercise program works the muscles that support the areas where injuries occur. Take particular care to include strength training for the muscles that support your forearms, upper arms, shoulders, and upper and lower legs.

A strength trainer will help you develop an individualized program. In the meantime, here are a few general guidelines. First, perform strength training two or three times a week, but never on successive days. The length of time you spend can range from 30 to 60 minutes per workout. Second, do one or two sets of each exercise. A set is accomplished when you perform the same exercise 8 to 15 times in succession with no rest. Perform 8 to 12 repetitions of each exercise using higher resistance to build strength and 12 to 15 repetitions of each exercise using lower resistance to build endurance.

Typically, people perform exercises that involve larger muscles at the beginning of a workout and progress to the smaller muscles. You may alternate upper- and lower-body exercises or do them on different days. Perhaps the most important principle to remember is that over time your body will adapt to the routine, and you will have to increase resistance by varying the weight you use, the number of repetitions, or number of sets.

The great thing about strength training is that you'll increase your metabolism and burn calories long after the workout is over. That helps control body weight. You'll also feel energized and improve your posture and overall appearance. It may not be your preferred activity, but 30 minutes of strength training two or three times a week is well worth the effort. It will allow you to play at a higher level and keep you on the tennis court for years to come.

If increasing strength through resistance training doesn't appeal to you, try yoga, Pilates, or martial arts training. These exercises can provide similar benefits. Just remember that strength training should be as specific as possible to the movements you make in tennis.

Improving Flexibility

Flexibility is the range of motion at a joint. It is not an overall body characteristic. Rather each joint has its own range of motion. You may be flexible when bending side to side but inflexible at your shoulder joint. Flexibility peaks in our 20s and from then, the decline begins.

As we age, flexibility declines because of the physiological changes to the structures of our joints: muscle, synovial fluid, and cartilage. With age, our joints often feel like they need a good squirt of oil, especially in the morning. Along with normal wear and tear, joints may also be susceptible to degenerative diseases such as osteoarthritis and osteoarthrosis. In fact, about 80 percent of the population between 55 and 64 years of age have signs of osteoarthritis in at least one joint. The good news is that physical activity is the primary remedy for loss of flexibility. Playing tennis can improve flexibility, but if it is your only physical activity, you may be heading for trouble.

The key to maintaining or improving your flexibility is static stretching exactly like the exercises shown in the section Cooling Down After Play (page 179). If you use these or similar static stretches each time you play tennis as part of your cool-down routine, you will likely maintain your existing flexibility. If you want to improve specific joint flexibility, consider adding daily static stretching.

Before performing static stretches, engage in a good general body warm-up to raise your body temperature and get blood flowing to muscles. You might also do a few dynamic stretches as part of your warm-up. Here are a few other guidelines for effective static stretching:

- Move slowly into static stretching positions and do not bounce, jerk, or force a stretch.
- Hold stretches for 15 to 30 seconds.
- Inhale as you start a stretch, exhale during the stretch, and breathe evenly while holding the stretch at its end position.
- While doing static stretches, proceed from the upper body, to the trunk, and finally to the lower body.

If static stretching isn't for you, consider yoga, Pilates, tai chi, dance, or aquatic exercise to improve specific joint flexibility. Whatever medium for flexibility training you choose, you'll reap the benefits of improved posture, less pain at joints, improved balance, and more efficient tennis play.

Enhancing Dynamic Balance

Balance is the process by which we control our body's center of mass, i.e., the balance point at which all body segments are evenly distributed. Maintaining balance while moving through space is referred to as *dynamic balance*. Playing tennis helps us maintain our ability to balance our body and retain mobility.

As we age, dynamic balance can be affected by a decline in some of the systems that enhance balance, such as vision, kinesthetic senses, or inner-ear equilibrium. We also may experience declining strength and flexibility unless we work to stop their deterioration. Taken together, these factors should illuminate the need to improve balance and stability on the court in order to play tennis safely.

When you play tennis, it is critical to keep your body's center of mass under control. This means moving with a stride length that does not extend your body too far in any direction. Long strides tend to put you out of balance, and smaller steps keep you centered.

Off the tennis court, use of an exercise ball can help you maintain body balance in a variety of positions. Just maintaining balance while sitting on the ball is helpful, and performing various stretches using the ball is even better. You might also use simple balancing boards or foam surfaces to challenge your body as you perform various movements.

An experienced tennis coach can help you assess your dynamic balance during play and suggest improvements. Minimize the habits of leaning,

Use an exercise ball to build strength and flexibility.

bending awkwardly, or backpedaling that you got away with in your 20s and 30s if you want to prevent injuries as you age.

Building a Team of Health Care Professionals

At this point, you may be puzzled or confused by some of the terms, advice, or directions in this chapter. If so, it's time to consult the experts. Over the years we've been fortunate to have the counsel and advice of health care professionals from various backgrounds to help us deal with caring for our bodies as athletes. Consider building a team of professionals who are familiar with the demands of tennis as a sport and are sensitive to your needs as a tennis player. Ask other players for references or ask a health care professional to recommend people they trust in complementary fields. The following are team members you might consider.

Your family physician is the key team member who has access to your overall health records and current health status. Depending on your health care insurance, you may need a referral from your primary care physician before you see another specialist, such as an orthopedic physician or physical therapist. An orthopedic physician with a specialty in sports medicine will be able to advise you on injuries to the bones, muscles, and joints. A physical therapist has the knowledge, skills, and equipment to help you recover from injuries in the shortest amount of time.

Other support professionals, such as a chiropractor and deep-tissue massage therapist, can help you stay limber. A chiropractor can adjust your spinal alignment periodically. A deep-tissue massage therapist will work on the fascia and muscle tissue to relieve tension and help them function smoothly. For long-term fitness, seek the advice of a professional strength trainer. A certified strength trainer can individualize a strength and flexibility training program for your particular needs.

We can attest to the excellent care and advice we've received over the years from health care professionals who helped keep us on the tennis court. Building your own team of health professionals will shorten your stay on the disabled list and keep your spirits high. Even better, use this team wisely to help you prevent injuries before they occur.

Preventing and Caring for Injuries

Nothing is more frustrating for active tennis players than physical injury. This can range from serious traumatic injuries to nagging overuse injuries that keep you off the tennis court for months at a time. But you can minimize the risk of injury through smart body management and care through strength, flexibility, and balance training. You can also make strategic and technical adjustments to your play that reduce the stress on your body every time you play.

A traumatic injury is the result of an incident such as a turned ankle. You know immediately that something is wrong. Overuse injuries are more subtle and may progress from an annoying slight pain to a full-scale problem caused by a repetitive movement. Both types can be debilitating. Smart management of the injury can get you back on the court sooner than trying to gut it out and play through the injury.

The classic advice for dealing with injuries is the acronym *PRICE*. That stands for *prevention, rest, ice, compression,* and *elevation*. For almost all injuries, this is the prescription to follow.

Prevention is obviously the best way to avoid injuries in the first place. Prevention includes warming up and cooling down and committing to a training plan for strength, flexibility, and balance like those described earlier in the chapter. It also implies using your best judgment when choosing equipment and shoes, when playing in the heat, and when determining the frequency and duration of each tennis outing.

Rest simply means that when something hurts, don't use it for fear of making the injury worse. Instead, get help from a health care professional and follow his or her advice. Over time, with active rest and rehabilitation, most injuries can be overcome. You know you have an injury if you experience any of the following: joint pain, tenderness at a specific point, swelling, reduced range of motion, weakness, or a feeling of numbness and tingling.

Ice is the best known initial treatment for almost any injury. Stay away from heat until well into the rehabilitation process, even if it feels good. Ice prevents swelling and keeps blood from pooling at the site of injury. Use crushed ice that can mold itself to the injured body part.

Compression works as a partner to ice to reduce swelling. If you injure an ankle, keep your tennis shoe on, wrap it with an elastic bandage, and apply ice. It's a great idea to include an elastic bandage or two in your tennis bag along with a plastic bag to hold ice. You never know when you or another player will need immediate help. Know where to get ice at your tennis facility, too, so there is no delay in treating a traumatic injury. Elevation is the third member of the team to combat swelling. Elevate the injured body part to draw fluid from the injury site.

We've seen many tennis players suffer an injury, take a few days off, and then get back on the court too soon. What a mistake. If the injury is not completely healed, it is just an accident waiting to happen. If the injury was caused by faulty technique, surely the technique hasn't improved from rest. And finally, during the resting phase, the player has probably lost strength and flexibility in the injured part from lack of use. All these signs point to another injury, probably more severe than the first one.

A better plan is to consult a health care specialist who can evaluate the injury, recommend care, and set up a plan for rehabilitation. Your body is clearly demanding help and objecting to the strain you've put it under. This is the time to fix faulty tennis technique, increase the strength of the surrounding muscles, and improve your flexibility. Listen to your body and the advice of an expert.

For many tennis injuries, the most logical expert to start with is an orthopedic surgeon who specializes in sports medicine. He or she is trained to treat injuries that occur through sports participation and is more likely than other physicians to be able to diagnose the injury correctly, pinpoint possible causes, and share your enthusiasm for returning to play as soon as possible. Search for a sports medicine physician online at www.aossm.org or contact the American Orthopaedic Society for Sports Medicine at 6300 N. River Road, Suite 500, Rosemont, Illinois, 60018.

After the initial diagnosis and care, a sports medicine physician may refer you to a physical therapist to rehabilitate the injury. Even though it may be inconvenient, you have to follow through on this phase of recovery to speed the healing process and strengthen the surrounding muscle groups. Before you return to play, ask your physical therapist whether protective braces or other devices could help protect the injury site. For example, with a tennis elbow injury, a counterforce brace on your forearm could reduce the shock of the ball hitting the racket. Stringing your racket at a lower tension could also help protect your elbow. Other joint issues could be supported by changing the type of shoes you wear or wearing a neoprene brace when you first return to play.

Once you've completed the medical rehabilitation, check in with your tennis professional if there is a possibility your injury was caused by tennis technique. There is little point in continuing to hit the tennis ball in a way that will eventually put you out of the game. Fix a faulty serve or backhand before you resume regular play.

Fueling the Body for Exercise

About two-thirds of the body is water, and water is second only to oxygen in importance to your body. By this stage of life, we hope you are well aware of the need to drink water throughout the day. When you play tennis, especially in the heat, water becomes critical.

Consuming water throughout the day helps rid your body of waste products and helps transport nutrients and hormones through your body. Without prescribing a specific amount of water to drink each day, let's just accept that the best policy for water consumption is to drink regularly and often.

Before you play tennis, drink several glasses of water to prepare your body for activity. During play, be sure to sip water at every changeover, even when you are not thirsty. Cool water will help reduce your body temperature and replace the fluids lost through perspiration. After play, replace the fluids lost through exercise and drink fluid with your postgame snack to aid in digestion.

Sports drinks can be an alternative to water, although many experts believe they often contain too much sugar or other substances. A better alternative is to drink a diluted sports drink, especially if you play in extreme heat. Sports drinks will help regulate your body's electrolyte balance and help restore energy to your body.

The bottom line is drink water every day and increase the amount you consume on days that you play tennis. During play, you absolutely must replace the fluid lost through perspiration to maintain optimum functioning. If you were brought up thinking that taking a drink is somehow a sign of weakness during athletic competition, get over it. Science has clearly shown that significant amounts of water consumption are essential before, during, and after activity.

Foods are the other fuel for your body to be considered. Without going into a lengthy discussion of nutrition strategies, the following are a few key ideas that will help you play your best tennis.

Eat light and often throughout the day to regulate your blood sugar and maximize energy. Even if you don't feel hungry, your body still needs fuel for daily living, especially during physical activity. Eat smaller portions of food every 3 to 4 hours throughout the day to prevent a drop in energy and blood sugar.

Consume healthy snacks of 100 to 150 calories between meals. Foods such as fresh fruit, nutrition bars, yogurt, hard-boiled eggs, nuts, and trail mix can be good choices. Check the labels on these products, because even nutrition bars can vary widely in the number of calories and the amount of fat and sugar.

These same foods are excellent choices for snacking during play to restore energy or between matches if you have to play several matches on one day. Be careful of high-glycemic foods such as candy bars, chips, and pretzels as snacks. These foods are quickly converted into blood glucose but dissipate quickly and after a quick burst of energy, leave you feeling tired and lethargic.

Your daily diet should contain about 40 percent grains, 40 percent fruits and vegetables, and 20 percent protein to maximize your body functions and energy. Eat a prematch meal about 2 hours before play. The best prematch meal is high in complex carbohydrate and low in fat and protein and includes plenty of water. Carbohydrate is the most efficient source of energy and is quickly digested and ready for use by the body.

After the match, similar rules apply. Eat a balanced light meal or snack within an hour of stopping play to replenish carbohydrate and fluids that are lost during physical activity.

WORDS TO THE WISE

- Work on your tennis technique with the assistance of a certified professional to help prevent injuries.
- Establish a ritual for warming up and cooling down every time you play tennis.
- Work on your overall body strength, flexibility, and balance to minimize the effects of aging, reduce the possibility of injury, and improve your tennis play.
- In case of injury, follow the PRICE principles but also enlist the help of a varied team of health care professionals who understand sports medicine.
- Fine-tune your racket technique with the help of an experienced, certified tennis professional to promote efficiency of movement and reduce the odds for an injury.
- Fuel your body with water and food so that you can perform at your optimal level.

The Tennis Lifestyle

Once we move into our fifth decade, most of us begin to make changes in our lifestyle. Perhaps you are a new empty nester, living in a house with no children for the first time in many years. Or you may be shifting into your retirement years by reducing the number of hours you spend at work. Likely, you are beginning to pay more attention to your personal health and fitness level as the realities of the aging process start to affect you.

Tennis can be the cornerstone of your lifestyle for the next several decades. Just how much time and energy you allocate to tennis activities is up to you. Our experience has convinced us that tennis can be great exercise, a competitive sport, a social experience, an excuse to travel, entertainment, and valuable family time. Each of these roles is significant individually, but when you combine and integrate them into your lifestyle, they can become a powerful anchor.

In this chapter, we explore scheduling regular tennis games for fun and exercise; adding spice with competitive tennis; making tennis a family affair; socializing and making friends through tennis; becoming a tennis fan; enjoying tennis events, travel, and vacations; and keeping tennis fun and fresh.

If tennis has been part of your lifestyle, you may want to consider ways to keep it fresh, exciting, and satisfying. We know groups of tennis players who brag about playing with the same group for decades, and then inevitably someone moves away or someone gets injured or faces a health problem

Playing tennis with your grandkids is a healthy way to bond.

and drops out. The sad result is that too often the others in the group also stop playing, much to their detriment.

Variety in your tennis life keeps the passion alive. Playing with different partners and against different opponents and adding mixed doubles to the recipe can be exhilarating. Join a group for drills and tips from a professional, take a Cardio Tennis class, or join a local league for players over 50.

Spend time with family and loved ones on the tennis court. Introduce your grandkids to the game and help them get started. At your facility, offer to hit with a promising junior player, such as the kid who always hangs around looking for someone to hit with.

If tennis has not been part of your lifestyle, figuring out how to start may seem daunting. So begin slowly, track your progress by setting monthly goals, and readjust them as you succeed. Begin with safe choices, perhaps with the help of a teaching professional in a series of four to eight group sessions to focus on strategy and technique of doubles play. At the same time, look for likely playing partners within your group or with friends you already know who play at a similar level. Here is where the tennis director or pro can help you find a good match for playing partners.

Surveys of people who dropped out of playing tennis over the years reveal the three most common excuses: not enough time, no one to play with, and lack of playing skill. In this chapter we help you solve each of these barriers and focus on your own goals for playing tennis. In some cases, you may need to adjust your attitude. In others, you may just need helpful advice or alternatives. Our goal is to share with you our experience from a personal standpoint and from years of watching thousands of tennis players.

Scheduling Regular Tennis Games for Fun and Exercise

The secret to sticking with an exercise program is to give it a high priority, schedule it well in advance, and give it up only grudgingly. In colder climates, court time is sold as seasonal time by the hour for periods of 30 to 40 weeks, payable in advance. Once you've plunked down the cash to play indoor tennis for a season, it is less likely you will cancel a game, especially if you have a frugal streak.

If you do not have to pay for court time in advance, arrange to play with a particular group or groups for a season. The season may depend on the weather, but 12 to 16 weeks is about right. That locks you in for a specific amount of time while allowing an escape to join other groups or rearrange group members.

If you've followed our advice in earlier chapters, you've developed potential playing partners through teaching clinics, team practices, or recommendations from your teaching professional. Compatible groups typically include players at similar National Tennis Rating Program (NTRP) levels with similar goals for balancing competition, exercise, and social interaction. Although you'll find a range of players at a similar skill level, conflicts may arise if some players are highly competitive and others are there to have fun, relax, and have a drink afterward.

When joining a group, don't be put off by differences in ages or even genders. Skill level and attitudes toward the purpose of play are more critical than artificial barriers. In fact, some of the most interesting foursomes we've played in have been those with a mix of ages, genders, and backgrounds.

It is up to your group to pick days and times to schedule play. In most groups one person becomes the leader or organizer for the group and arranges the weekly games. Some groups even schedule an entire season of play with weeks off and a plan for substitutes when players are unavailable. A list of potential substitutes is essential because one member of the group or more will invariably be unavailable.

We know from personal experience that e-mail contact within a group works best. Telephone calls are annoying and time consuming, and there are too many missed calls. The group leader simply sends out a schedule for play each week, players respond, and everything is confirmed by e-mail.

You can be a popular group member by responding to invitations promptly, arriving on time to play, supplying tennis balls when it is your turn, being mentally prepared to play, and enjoying yourself as part of the group. Failure in any of these areas makes finding future groups and partners risky.

Setting personal priorities is never easy, but you and your spouse or significant other should agree on the importance of your regular tennis games and stick by it. We've developed the habit of scheduling other things in life around our tennis to make sure we keep our commitment to ourselves, each other, and our health and fitness.

Adding Spice With Competitive Tennis

Although you may prefer tennis for exercise, fun, and socializing, don't completely rule out competitive tennis. Adding the element of competition beyond your normal game adds excitement, interest, and variety to your routine. With a little experimentation, you can find a level of competition that suits you.

Start with your local tennis facility. Consider joining a competitive round-robin or a seasonlong league among facility members. Some clubs offer annual club tournaments or member–guest tournaments.

Playing on a local team for people 50 and over or in a Unites States Tennis Association (USTA) adult league can be a terrific experience. You'll meet

Photo courtesy of Lee Godwin

The USTA offers fun, competitive options for tennis players over 50.

new people and a variety of characters and enjoy challenging yourself as well. Team practices can be great fun, motivating, and socially enjoyable. If your team does well locally, you may qualify for state, sectional, and national championships sponsored by the USTA. Teams that qualify usually report that these events are a once-in-a-lifetime opportunity.

All of these local and USTA leagues are offered at specific NTRP levels, so you'll compete against other players at your level. Most 50-plus leagues concentrate on doubles play, although some offer singles. Mixed doubles for players 50 and older is also an enticing opportunity for many people.

Making Tennis a Family Affair

When we were married, instead of the traditional rehearsal dinner, we hosted a tennis party at an indoor tennis club for our family and friends. I guess that tells you a little about our network of family and friends and our commitment to sharing our passion for tennis with our loved ones, which continues to this day.

In our network, it is not important how well you play tennis but the fact that you have played and enjoy the game. We've also played lots of Wiffle

© 2008 Ben Boyd

Make tennis a family affair.

ball and touch football in our family, but as all of us have aged and experienced various ailments and infirmities, those sports have abated while tennis still survives. Eventually, we may convert to golf as some family members have done, but not until we're too old for tennis.

You can give your kids, nieces, nephews, and grandchildren a memorable gift by introducing them to the sport of tennis. Do it gradually by letting them watch you play, providing a children's racket, and encouraging their first efforts to hit the ball.

Most kids aren't ready to play tennis until they can throw and catch a ball consistently. By age five or six, if they can track a ball and catch it, they are ready to try to strike a tennis ball. First attempts should be trying to strike a balloon or soft foam ball that is larger than a tennis ball. Don't worry about hitting over a net; just help them learn basic racket skills such as hitting ups and downs, having a self-rally with a bounce, and eventually hitting back and forth with you across a distance of no more than 6 feet (1.8 meters).

When a child has some success controlling the ball, have her try hitting over a small net from a distance no more than 6 feet (1.8 meters). That will help control the hits and maximize the chances of keeping the ball in play.

If the kids encounter success, it's time to sign them up for a group session or summer tennis camp. Check out local options with instructors who

When teaching tennis to your grandkids, rally with an oversized foam ball at first.

are dedicated to making tennis fun, and help arrange the opportunity. Lots of grandparents, aunts, and uncles help with the costs, too, because the parents may not be able to absorb another expense.

Socializing and Making Friends Through Tennis

It is impossible to generalize about the types of people who play tennis, because they come in all shapes, sizes, ages, and income levels. Once you get into the game, you'll meet terrific people and likely find some you enjoy socializing with both on and off the tennis court.

Studies of aging patterns have shown that as we age, we seek new social relationships. For many of us, the workplace provides a social network and outlet. But once we leave an employer, particularly if we relocate to another city, we also lose much of our social network. When we had children at home, their school functions provided many of our social contacts as well, but once children have grown, we're on our own for building a social network.

Socializing and drinks with friends after play.

Joining a tennis group at a facility is one of the fastest ways to make new friends and expand your social network. We've noticed over the years that tennis facilities that have a comfortable spot for relaxing and socializing after play provide the best overall experience for tennis, particularly if healthy snacks and drinks are available. The camaraderie and verbal sparring after a match are a terrific bonus added to the playing time.

Take time after you play to get to know your playing partners and other players who are present. You'll meet great people and make helpful business contacts and personal connections with other potential playing partners. If you simply play tennis and leave abruptly, you're missing a prime opportunity to add to your network of friends.

After a season of play, many tennis groups get together for a culminating activity, usually built around food and drinks. Include spouses so that they become part of the network and can meet the people you play tennis with each week. We've joined tennis friends at concerts, plays, book clubs, Cirque du Soleil, baseball games, and tennis exhibitions by Sampras and Courier just in the past two years as newcomers to a community. We've also benefited from referrals for health insurance, physicians, massage therapists, dentists, chiropractors, computer technicians, and, of course, lots of restaurants.

Some of our best memories and friendships developed from playing tennis and joining a group of players for a late dinner or snack afterward. More than 25 years later, we still count those people as friends, even though most of us have dispersed throughout the country.

Becoming a Tennis Fan

Playing tennis is more fun than watching others play, but we also enjoy being tennis fans. We never miss the late rounds of the Grand Slams of professional tennis: the U.S. Open, Wimbledon, the French Open, and the Australian Open. Nothing gets us more excited to play than watching great players compete. We also enjoy watching local high school matches, college matches, and even junior competitive events. It's fun to watch younger players who are still exploring their limits test themselves, deal with pressure, and invent new strategies to try to win a match.

A good first step to becoming a tennis fan is to join the United States Tennis Association. For a modest membership fee, you receive monthly issues of *Tennis* magazine along with other regular mailings. Your membership entitles you to play in USTA League Tennis or age group tournaments. At the very least, log on to www.usta.com for the latest tennis news and advice for free.

The USTA is the governing body for tennis in the United States, designated by the United States Olympic Committee and endorsed by the U.S. Congress. About 85 percent of the revenue generated by the USTA each year comes from the 14-day U.S. Open held at the Billie Jean King National Tennis Center in Flushing Meadows, New York. Virtually all of that revenue, upwards of $150 million, goes back to promoting the game of tennis in the United States.

In many parts of the country, the Tennis Channel is available on cable television. Programming is varied, and, along with offering professional tennis, the channel provides instructional programs, player interviews and profiles, and updates on tennis news and equipment.

Finally, you might want to follow the careers of your favorite players on the professional tours by logging onto the Web sites for the men at www.atptennis.com and women at www.sonyericssonwtatour.com. Both Web sites offer player profiles, tournament results, and human interest stories beyond what you can view on television. You might also enjoy the tennis blogs, fantasy tennis play, equipment advice, and tennis statistics of all types.

a   *b*

Follow the careers of your favorite professional players: *(a)* **Roger Federer and** *(b)* **Maria Sharapova have both won Grand Slam championships.**

Enjoying Tennis Events, Travel, and Vacations

If you are an active, passionate tennis fan, you might enjoy attending various tennis events, traveling to tennis-related sites, or just taking a tennis vacation. You can find lots of opportunities on the Internet or by reading monthly issues of *Tennis* magazine.

USTA sections or community tennis associations often stage local tennis events to promote the sport. They may offer live entertainment, free clinics, or a tennis exhibition. Local communities often feature tennis tournaments hosted by a group to raise money for charity. At these events, local teaching professionals often donate their time as playing partners for people like you who donate money to the charity. If you want the thrill of an excellent doubles partner, these events might be for you.

College tennis matches can also be exciting events whether you attend them occasionally or as a regular booster. Check out match times at local colleges and watch some excellent tennis and great team competition. College teams now play the doubles matches first, and then follow with singles play, so plan your trip accordingly.

Photo courtesy of the University of Illinois

College tennis produces exciting, passionate tennis, and often admission is free.

At the professional level, the Grand Slam tournaments are the ultimate experience. Each one is set in a unique atmosphere that distinguishes it from any other event. There is nothing quite like a week in Paris, London, New York, or Melbourne taking in the matches and enjoying the rich cultural experiences in the city. Friends of ours have made it their goal to attend every Grand Slam event and have enjoyed each one more than the last.

For a different tennis treat, you also might enjoy a Davis Cup or Fed Cup team match between two countries. The natural patriotism and the partisan home crowd make these team competitions unique to professional tennis players and produce thrilling, unpredictable results.

Two sources for tennis event travel are Championship Tennis Tours (www.tennistours.com) or Grand Slam Tennis Tours (www.grandslamtennistours.com). Consider organizing a group of your own so that you will know your travel companions, and you may be able to offset your costs by recruiting others.

Vacations to fine resorts and exotic locations can be a dream come true for tennis aficionados. Look to the Caribbean, the south of France, or anywhere in the world to find amazing tennis resorts. If you're more focused on the United States, turn to recommendations from *Tennis* magazine by accessing their Web site at www.tennis.com. Look under travel for a listing of the top 50 tennis resorts. The magazine also ranks resorts according to best lodging, food, and spas and which offer the strongest teaching programs, best partner matching, or programs for families. These rankings are updated annually, and don't you pity the poor souls who have to travel to each of these sites to rate them?

Finally, if your travels take you to New England, the International Tennis Hall of Fame in Newport, Rhode Island, is an enticing stopover. It houses an exhibit of the history of the game in an attractive facility. You can also sign up to play on the facility's famous grass tennis courts. Newport is a charming town full of historic mansions of the rich and famous from yesteryear. It sits on a lovely coastline and features art and jazz during the summer season.

Keeping Tennis Fun and Fresh

We guess you could tire of tennis after several years, but we haven't. The secret may be in expanding our circle of friends, partners, and experiences and keeping up with new trends in the game. It's not the same game it was 25 years ago, but then neither are we the same people.

Today's tennis has new stars, new fashions, better court surfaces, remarkable new racket technology, and more comfortable clothing in dazzling colors. Tennis shoes are better made and last longer, tennis balls are still a bargain, and we now know that drinking water during a match is smart.

Prize money is at an all-time high, the Grand Slam tournaments are thriving and profitable, and men and women receive equal prize money on the professional tours. Tie-breaks provide excitement and suspense and end the misery of interminable matches. High definition, blue courts, and yellow tennis balls make watching tennis on television dramatically different from in the past. Short shorts are out, sleeveless shirts are in, and tennis fashions will keep changing.

No matter which activity you enjoy, time off from that activity is essential. If you're tired of arranging matches, bored with your tennis group, maxed out on lessons, or frustrated by your level of play, take a break. Chances are you'll come back to the game eager again, or you'll figure out a way to rejuvenate your game during the hiatus. A few weeks away from any activity is good and prevents burnout from the sameness of a routine. Keep tennis fun for you and your friends by doing the following:

- Treat yourself to a new racket.
- Join a new group or team.
- Socialize regularly with your tennis buddies.
- Take a tennis vacation.
- Share tennis with friends or family who are new to the game.
- Work on your body off the court so that you are stronger, more flexible, and better balanced.
- Pick a favorite player and follow him or her for the entire year. Maybe the Bryan twins?
- Join a competitive USTA adult league 50-plus team.
- Play mixed doubles.
- Take a tennis lesson or clinic from a teaching professional.
- Donate your time or money to a nonprofit foundation that provides tennis programs for kids.
- Watch a wheelchair tennis match. Be amazed.
- Support tennis by promoting it to anyone you meet.

WORDS TO THE WISE

- Commit yourself to a regularly scheduled tennis game and honor the commitment. Take time to socialize and swap stories after play.
- Consider adding a competitive tennis experience sometime during the next year.
- Introduce family and friends to tennis and nurture their interest as players, fans, or supporters.
- Enlarge your circle of friends and acquaintances through tennis contacts.
- Become a tennis fan when you're not on the court.
- Keep tennis new, fresh, and exciting by scheduling a trip or vacation or attending tennis events.
- Avoid tennis burnout by taking off a few weeks a year to do other things.

BIBLIOGRAPHY

Blackburn, G. 2001. Exercise: How much is enough? http://www.clevelandclinic.org/heartcenter/pub/guide/prevention/exercise/howmuchisenough.htm. Accessed 3/12/08.

Blaskower, P. 1993. *The art of doubles*. Cincinnati, OH: Betterway Books.

Brody, H. 1987. *Tennis science for tennis players*. Philadelphia: University of Pennsylvania Press.

Carr, G. 1997. *Mechanics of sport*. Champaign, IL: Human Kinetics.

Danish, S. 1990. *American youth and sports participation*. North Palm Beach, FL: Athletic Footwear Association.

Dick's Sporting Goods. 2008. How to buy a tennis racquet. http://www.dickssportinggoods.com/sm-tennis-racquet-buyers-guide--bg-222916.html.

Garrick, J., and P. Radetsky. 1986. *Peak condition*. New York: Crown Publishers.

Groppel, J.L., J.E. Loehr, D.S. Melville, and A.M. Quinn. 1989. *Science of coaching tennis*. Champaign, IL: Human Kinetics.

Jones, J. and D. Rose, eds. 2005. *Physical activity instruction for older adults*. Champaign, IL: Human Kinetics.

Jordan, R. 1999. *Tennis for winners*. King of Prussia, PA: Aconitum Press.

Kauss, D. 1980. *Peak performance*. Englewood Cliffs, NJ: Prentice-Hall.

Launder, A. 2001. *Play practice: The games approach to teaching and coaching sports*. Champaign, IL: Human Kinetics.

Milner, C. 2002. Motivating the 50+ adult. *Journal on Active Aging*. (Nov–Dec): 28–33.

Payne, G., and L. Isaacs. 2005. *Human motor development*. 6th ed. New York: McGraw-Hill. p. 439.

Roetert, P. and J. Groppel, eds. 2001. *World-class tennis technique*. Champaign, IL: Human Kinetics.

Roetert, P. and T. Ellenbecker. 2007. *Complete conditioning for tennis*. Champaign, IL: Human Kinetics.

Saviano, N. 2003. *Maximum tennis*. Champaign, IL: Human Kinetics.

Smith, S. 2002. *Stan Smith's winning doubles*. Champaign, IL: Human Kinetics.

Stroia, K. 2007. Total tennis workout. *Tennis*. (June): 74–79.

Talbert, W. and B. Old. 1968. *The game of doubles in tennis*. 3rd ed. Philadelphia: J.B. Lippincott.

United States Tennis Association. n.d. General and experienced player guidelines: Supplement to the NTRP guidelines. http://dps.usta.com/usta_master/usta/doc/content/doc_13_7372.pdf?12/6/2004%204:12:22%20PM .

United States Tennis Association. 1996. *Tennis tactics: Winning patterns of play*. Champaign, IL: Human Kinetics.

United States Tennis Association. 2000. *Friend at court*. New York: H.O. Zimman.

United States Tennis Association. 2003. *USTA tennis guide to dynamic and static stretching*. White Plains, NY: USTA.

United States Tennis Association. 2004. *Coaching tennis successfully*. 2nd ed. Champaign, IL: Human Kinetics.

United States Tennis Association. 2005. *A coaches' guide and curriculum for 50+ tennis players*. White Plains, NY: USTA.

Weinberg, R. and D. Gould. 1995. *Foundations of sport and exercise psychology*. Champaign, IL: Human Kinetics.

Westcott W. and T. Baechle. 2007. *Strength training past 50*. Champaign, IL: Human Kinetics.

INDEX

Note: The italicized *t* and *f* following page numbers refer to tables and figures, respectively.

ABOUT THE AUTHORS

Kathy Woods served as president of the United States Professional Tennis Association (USPTA) from 1994 to 1996, the first and only female to serve the association in that capacity. Founded in 1927, the USPTA is the world's oldest and largest nonprofit trade and certifying association for tennis teaching professionals. Currently, she is the director of tennis at the highly regarded Racquet Club of St. Petersburg. A certified teaching professional for almost 30 years, Woods has directed tennis programs in Princeton, New Jersey; Key Biscayne, Florida; and Westport, Connecticut. She has been a featured speaker for the International Tennis Federation at the Worldwide Coaches Workshop, the Japanese Professional Tennis Association, the USTA National Tennis Teachers Conference, and many regional workshops and conferences. In 1996, she was honored with the prestigious Educational Merit Award by the International Tennis Hall of Fame for outstanding service in tennis at the national level. As a competitive player, she earned a coveted Gold Ball by winning the USTA National 30s Doubles championships and has been ranked first in the nation by the USPTA in both singles and doubles. Woods played varsity tennis and graduated summa cum laude from the University of Pennsylvania.

Ron Woods, PhD, is a performance coach for the Human Performance Institute in Orlando, Florida, and an adjunct professor of sport science at the University of South Florida and the University of Tampa. He spent 20 years with the United States Tennis Association, serving as director of the community tennis programs with a major focus on the USA Tennis Plan for Growth, a massive project to increase tennis participation in the United States. He also initiated the USTA Welcome Back to Tennis campaign for players over age 50. For the 10 years prior to that, Ron was the USTA's director of player development, a program that develops top junior players into touring professional players. Earlier in his career, Woods was professor of physical education and men's tennis coach at West Chester University for 17 years. During his time at West Chester, he also served as dean of the School of Health, Physical Education, Recreation, and Athletics. He has been inducted into West Chester University's Athletic Hall of Fame. A graduate of East Stroudsburg University and an inductee into their Athletic Hall of Fame, Woods received his PhD from Temple University with an emphasis in sport psychology and motor learning. The International Tennis Hall of Fame awarded Ron the Educational Merit Award in 1997. He was also honored by the USPTA as National Coach of the Year in 1982 and named a master professional in 1984. His accomplishments include eight years on the coaching committee of the United States Olympic Committee and the Coaches' Commission of the International Tennis Association. Woods authored *Social Issues in Sport* and has written and edited numerous USTA publications, including *Coaching Youth Tennis*, *Tennis Tactics,* and *Coaching Tennis Successfully*, all published by Human Kinetics.

A mixed doubles team for over 30 years—and also husband and wife— Kathy and Ron Woods live in St. Petersburg, Florida.